❧ THE WARBURGS

❦ THE

WARBURGS

The Story of a Family

DAVID FARRER

STEIN AND DAY/*Publishers*/New York

First published in 1975

Copyright © 1974 by David Farrer

Library of Congress Catalog Card No. 74-78541

All rights reserved

Designed by Ed Kaplin

Printed in the United States of America

Stein and Day/*Publishers*/Scarborough House, Briarcliff Manor, N.Y. 10510

ISBN 0-8128-1733-8

To Harry and Val, my companions in so much

AUTHOR'S NOTE

Unless otherwise noted all quotations or personal accounts
by individual Warburgs are from private
conversations with the author over the last several
years, or from private papers, still in family hands,
and unavailable to the public.

ACKNOWLEDGMENTS

I want to make clear that this book was not commissioned by any member of the Warburg family.

The Warburgs, in fact, is published without the family's blessing. Nonetheless, I would like to express my gratitude for the interviews granted to me by many members of the family. I was particularly fortunate in being allowed to inspect and read a great number of unpublished memoirs, archives, and papers. I am also indebted to Professor E. H. Gombrich, head of the Warburg Institute in London, Mr. Maurice Dexter, the late Mr. Joseph Barnes, Mr. Geoffrey Hellman, Mr. George Oppenheimer, and to Mr. Jacob Marcus, the director of the American Jewish Archives at the Hebrew Union College, Cincinnati, for permission to examine the Felix Warburg papers.

I must also thank Mr. Brock Baker for valuable editorial assistance, Mr. Toby Eady for his constant encouragement, and Mrs. Robert Henriques, in whose lovely Cotswold house much of the first draft of this book was written.

❧ Contents

THE WARBURGS

Contents

List of Illustrations

❧ Introduction

In the history of Western Europe over the last two hundred years, the names of certain families have acquired a kind of magic: the Churchills, for example, the Kennedys, the Rockefellers, and the Rothschilds—they are household words. Without knowing exactly why, we want to know every detail about them—about their most spectacular successes and their most trivial domestic arrangements; their powerful friends and what we fondly imagine are their equally powerful passions. The name Warburg has never had the same ring about it. Though eminent—even preeminent—in many fields over the last two centuries, the Warburgs have never excited quite the same degree of curiosity.

Yet from the day in the first half of the sixteenth century when the family's common ancestor, Simon von Cassel, emerged from the mists of total obscurity to knock on the gates of the town of Warburg in German Westphalia, the Warburgs have displayed a tremendous range of talents in many countries. One writer, in a profile of the family published some years ago,[1] listed twenty-nine occupations pursued by individual members in an equal number of countries over the last four hundred years:

[1]Geoffrey T. Hellman, "A Schiff Sortie and a Warburg Wallaw or, Churning around with the Churnagooses," *The New Yorker*, 11, June, 1955.

saddlemaker	animal slaughterman
merchant	shawl manufacturer
banker	tobacconist
bookseller	naval officer
horsehair dealer	musician
clock manufacturer	soldier
book censor	photographer
art critic	company director
wool dyer	doctor
author	librarian
consul	editor
paper manufacturer	naturalist
stationer	professor
ribbon merchant	composer
joiner (wholesale)	

This book is primarily concerned with the main branch of the family, the branch that moved in the eighteenth century from the tiny town of Warburg to Danish Altona and from there to the wider horizons of Hamburg. This branch (the Warburg stem of Jesse—see genealogical tree,) has included the chief architect of the Federal Reserve System in the United States, the founders (and their descendants) of the wealthiest banking firm in Germany, and a man who revitalized the operations of the City of London. In addition, the family has given us one of the greatest of all art historians, a Nobel prize winner, and several important confidantes of three U.S. presidents.

Simon von Cassel and his immediate descendants realized that money was the only guarantee of safety in whatever society they were living. As was the case for most Jews up to the beginning of the nineteenth century moneylending was the only profession open to them. But the Warburgs were to some extent an exception: Almost from the start they regarded moneylending less as an end than as a means to a fuller participation in society.

Early Warburgs were lucky to start their family fortune in a comparatively enlightened town like Warburg. Its Jews were regarded as second-class citizens but were never persecuted and were not forced to live in a ghetto. Still, even in Warburg, and certainly in the rest of Germany, it was not until the nineteenth century that a Jew could feel safe, much less accepted.

So, slowly and prudently, money they sought and, since they combined complete honesty with an innate financial sense, money they gained. In due course the family was able to enjoy what their less able Gentile countrymen took for granted—political and economic security. It was at this point that the genius that was inherent in them could begin to be expressed. At the same time, though, there emerged what proved to be a continuing paradox. While striving individually and collectively for great achievements, members of the family have often seemed reluctant to seek or even accept public acclaim. And so the Warburg chrysalis has never produced to the public the multiple butterflies that would have made the name Warburg—like Churchill, Rockefeller, and Rothschild—one to conjure with. It is one of the aims of this book to remedy that state of affairs.

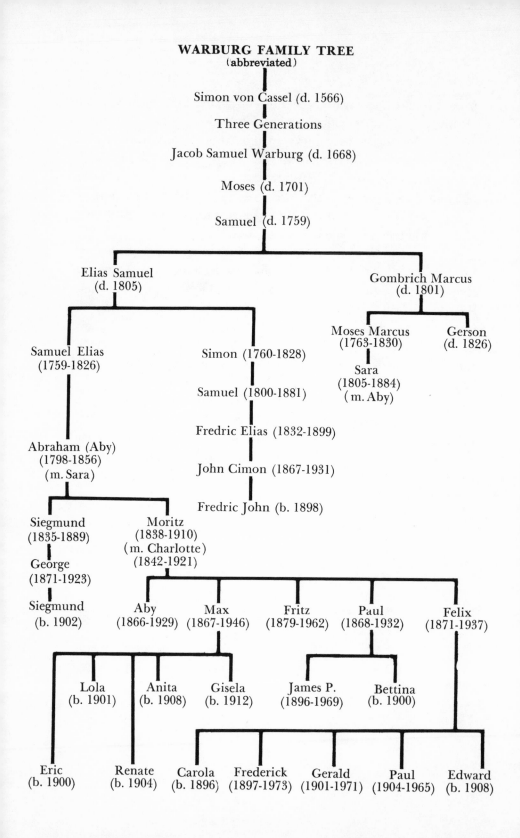

WARBURG FAMILY TREE
(abbreviated)

Simon von Cassel (d. 1566)

Three Generations

Jacob Samuel Warburg (d. 1668)

Moses (d. 1701)

Samuel (d. 1759)

Elias Samuel
(d. 1805)

Gombrich Marcus
(d. 1801)

Samuel Elias
(1759-1826)

Simon (1760-1828)

Moses Marcus
(1763-1830)

Gerson
(d. 1826)

Samuel (1800-1881)

Sara
(1805-1884)
(m. Aby)

Fredric Elias (1832-1899)

Abraham (Aby)
(1798-1856)
(m. Sara)

John Cimon (1867-1931)

Fredric John (b. 1898)

Siegmund
(1835-1889)

Moritz
(1838-1910)
(m. Charlotte)
(1842-1921)

George
(1871-1923)

Siegmund
(b. 1902)

Aby
(1866-1929)

Max
(1867-1946)

Fritz
(1879-1962)

Paul
(1868-1932)

Felix
(1871-1937)

Lola
(b. 1901)

Anita
(b. 1908)

Gisela
(b. 1912)

James P.
(1896-1969)

Bettina
(b. 1900)

Eric
(b. 1900)

Renate
(b. 1904)

Carola
(b. 1896)

Frederick
(1897-1973)

Gerald
(1901-1971)

Paul
(1904-1965)

Edward
(b. 1908)

❧ THE WARBURGS

CHAPTER ONE

The Beginnings

TRADITION has it that the town of Warburg was founded as Warburgum by Charlemagne in 778. Today it is the chief—indeed the only—town of *Landkreis* ("district") Warburg, soon to be swallowed up by the neighboring and swiftly expanding industrial center of Paderborn.

Warburg climbs up the face of a high hill on the eastern border of Westphalia. At its foot flows the sleepy little Diemel River. Near its summit stand the fourteenth-century church of St. John and the Rathaus completed in 1560. Close by are the Erasmus Chapel, with a twelfth-century crypt, and (built somewhat later) the four round watchtowers of the Dominican monastery. The streets of the lower town are still rife with heavily timbered medieval houses. The views are panoramically peaceful in every direction. You look out over richly wooded or green countryside, and though recently a few light industries have been established in the town's outskirts, agriculture is still, as it has been for nearly a thousand years, the basis of the community's existence.

The earliest extant records of Warburg's existence date from A.D. 1001. For more than four hundred years subsequent to its founding there were, in effect, two separate Warburgs—the upper and lower towns led independent existences. Then by mutual agreement the two became one, celebrating the event by building the Rathaus (completed one hundred years later), which straddled the previous border between them.

The Warburg community prospered in the wool trade and became known for its excellent beer. You can still drink a pint of Warburg. But neither the town nor its chief citizens made any real mark on history.

Today Warburg is little changed. It has the air of a Rip van Winkle town. It seems a strange place to have given its name to a famous family. Nevertheless, in the sixteenth century a Jew by the name of Simon von Cassel arrived in its sleepy precincts.

Simon von Cassel is the first known ancestor of the Warburg family. He is the root from which has stemmed and branched a family tree of enormous ramifications which today fills a sizable volume. Where Simon's forebears came from is uncertain, but the family has always maintained that it is Sephardic in origin.

According to the Warburgs, their ancestors followed in the wake of the all-conquering converts of Muhammad as they ranged along the coast of North Africa and across the Strait of Gibraltar into Europe, settling in the Iberian peninsula. Driven out of Spain by the persecutions of Ferdinand and Isabella in the late fifteenth century, they settled in the Lombardy plain of Northern Italy.

Though there is no written evidence of these migrations, the frequency with which the patronym Delbanco crops up in their early authenticated story appears to confirm at least their Italian sojourn.

But with the emergence of Simon von Cassel from the mists of time and uncertainty, we are on relatively firm ground. It *is* certain that the Simon who sought accommodations in Warburg came from neighboring Cassel.

In the sixteenth century, and for long afterward, the Jews in Germany were allowed no surnames; they could identify themselves only by means of the town in which they were allowed to live. Thus the "von" in those days was anything but honorific. It is only an agreeable legend that when they left Warburg the family took their name from the town that had treated them well. They had no alternative; when they moved on they could only identify themselves by the name of the place they had come from. So Simon von Cassel came to Warburg. Once he became established there, he and his descendants became (von) Warburgs.

In the town register Simon is described as "money changer, pawnbroker, and lender of funds against grain." He was allowed to settle in his new home by permission of the prince-bishop of Paderborn, under whose jurisdiction the town came. A *Schutzvertrag* ("protective agreement") guaranteed Simon safe residence for ten years.

The ten years stretched to a century, during which, according to what records remain, the family apparently prospered—in a mild way. But Warburg in the seventeenth century was a backwater. The chances for much financial advancement were slender.

Nonetheless, Simon and his descendants did possess one advantage denied to the greater number of their fellow Jews in Central and Eastern Europe. Though the Jews of the Paderborn prince-bishopric were certainly regarded as inferior citizens and were a community apart, with their own synagogue and cemetery (which can still be seen, lovingly tended, today), there is no record of their having been persecuted. Whatever their experience before arriving in Germany, the Warburgs of Warburg never knew the tribulations of a ghetto life such as were inflicted upon many Jews elsewhere in Europe.

But even Simon's ancestors had almost certainly escaped persecution, for in their treatment of the Jews of the Diaspora the Muslims had shown far greater tolerance than their Christian counterparts. The ghettos, and all they signified in hardship and degradation, originated not on the North African coastline nor the Iberian peninsula but in Europe east of the River Rhine.

Very different was the initial lot of the Rothschilds, who appeared on the German scene more than a century later. In his history *The Rothschilds*, Frederick Morton writes of Mayer

Rothschild, a native of Frankfurt and the real founder of the dynasty, returning to the city after a stay in the ghetto-free town of Hanover.

When he re-entered Frankfurt that spring day, not a shred of grandeur greeted him, only petty humiliation. Crossing the river Main, he had to pay Jew toll. . . . The ghetto brimmed along a single dark alley, just twelve feet broad. . . .

On his way Mayer could not escape the street urchins whose favorite amusement was to shout, "Jew, do your duty!"—whereupon the Jew had to step aside, take off his hat, and bow. Having thus entertained the local children, Mayer reached the heavy chains with which soldiers manacled the Judengasse (Jew Street) every night.[1]

In their German origins the Warburgs were more fortunate, but perhaps the ghetto gave the Rothschilds a greater impetus. Fear and uncertainty, which touched the Warburgs comparatively lightly, can be great spurs to achievement.

In the second half of the seventeenth century the Warburgs were on the move, and one Jacob Samuel emigrated to Altona in 1668. An incidental result of the move was the removal of that far-from-honorific "von." For Altona in the seventeenth century, though bordering the Hanseatic League port of Hamburg, was an autonomous principality acknowledging the overlordship of the kingdom of Denmark, and the Danes had an exceptionally liberal attitude toward Jews. The stigma of "von" was not required in Altona. The family would be known from then on simply as Warburg.

With the move to Altona the story of the Warburg family really begins.[2]

---

[1] Frederick Morton, *The Rothschilds* (New York: Atheneum, 1961), p. 16.

[2] The town of Warburg reappeared once in the family's history when Max Warburg, by then head of the Hamburg banking firm of M. M. Warburg & Co., was

All living members of the main branches of the family tree—the German, American, British, and Scandinavian—are directly descended from Jacob Samuel. He was one of the first German Jews to settle in Altona. They had been preceded perhaps a hundred years earlier by a group of Portuguese Jews. If in fact the Warburgs were of Portuguese origin, they had chosen a roundabout way of being reunited with their Portuguese "cousins."

The count of the county of Pinneburg, in which Altona was situated, had granted permission in 1584 to twenty Portuguese-Jewish families to settle in his domain. These families then requested a ban on further immigration. If they were to be made to pay taxes, they must be allowed to make money, they argued. There would be scant opportunity to do so in an unproductive land if Jewish entry were not severely restricted.

By 1641 Pinneburg had passed to the Danish throne, and the king made a new agreement with the Jews. He lifted the restriction on the numbers entering not only Altona but the whole of Denmark. They were also given permission to settle their disputes in their own rabbinical law courts, allowed their own cemetery, and perhaps most important, their own—Torah-influenced—schools.

It was into this society that Jacob Samuel came. He lost no time in establishing himself in his new surroundings. At his death in 1668 he had become leader of the Jewish High German community.[3]

At this time the commercial interests of Altona and the much larger city of Hamburg were identical, but a political boundary divided them. Altona was Danish, Hamburg was a free city, a

given the title of honorary president of the Warburg fire brigade. In return he gave them new fire equipment. Hopes of a greater "touch" may have inspired the burgomaster to grant the Warburg family the right to bear the seal of *Stadt Warburg* (a fleur-de-lis) as their coat of arms.

[3] In the Jewish cemetery of Altona the headstones for Jacob Samuel and his wife still exist. It is a dankly gloomy, tree-covered area, notable for the fact that the German headstones, for no known reason, stand upright, while the Portuguese lie prone on the ground.

member of the powerful Hanseatic League. It was Denmark, not Hamburg, that gave the Warburgs their first impetus along the road to commercial success.

Danish law forbade any Jew to use the title "banker" in describing his business, but this restriction was more honored in the breach than the observance. They might still be moneylenders in name, but in practice these Altona Warburgs became merchants —and then merchant bankers.

A grandson of Jacob Samuel founded the firm of S. G. Warburg in Altona in 1774, and two of his sons enlarged the business, which then became known as W. S. Warburg.

The next generation combined commerce with politics. One brother represented the province of Schleswig-Holstein in first the Danish and after 1864 the Prussian House of Deputies. Another, Pius, combined his political activities as a member of the provincial assembly with his love of music. Wherever politics took him he insisted that the authorities arrange for him a string quartet in which he himself could perform. Another frequent performer in these "house concerts" was Pius's old friend Johannes Brahms. At his death Pius left a fine collection of pictures to the Altona museum.

The Warburg firm in Altona remained independent if unremarkable all through the nineteenth century, but in 1907 it sold out to its by now famous Hamburg relatives, M. M. Warburg & Co.

Hamburg, as the eighteenth century drew to its close, offered opportunities for gain denied to the smaller Altona, and its attitude toward Jews had become less restrictive than was the case elsewhere in Germany. To Hamburg in 1773 came Marcus Gombrich Warburg, and in that city in 1798 his two sons, Moses Marcus and Gerson, founded the firm of M. M. Warburg and Sons.

There were stormy early years for the firm—whose owners were still known only as *Geldwechsler* ("money-changers"). The shadow of Napoleon was falling on Europe, and in 1804 Hamburg was besieged by the French army. A cousin of the two brothers, Elias Samuel, was ordered by the authorities to work out how long Hamburg could hold out. He predicted the very day of the city's fall, and on that day he collapsed and died.

On entering the city, Napoleon seized Gerson as a hostage. His brother showed a marked reluctance to contribute to the sum needed from the Jewish community to secure Gerson's release. Only under extreme pressure from his fellow Jews did he pay up, and then not to the extent that had been expected of him.

Whatever differences Marcus's reluctance to pay his brother's ransom suggested, a few years later, in 1810, the brothers signed an unconditional deed of partnership.

Written mainly in Hebrew, with an admixture of even older Aramaic words, it concludes:

AND BECAUSE WE ARE MEN and the day when we shall be called to God is hidden from the living, so it shall be that when one of us dies there shall be no Rabbinical Tribunal, no community and no trustee to intervene and disturb the routine by inquiries, but the surviving brother shall be the only heir.

This deed should perhaps be seen not only as a burying of the hatchet but also as an assurance that personal vendettas should not in future be allowed to affect business interests or weaken Warburg family solidarity in the face of a potentially hostile world.

The withdrawal of the French in 1814 afforded new opportunities for the recently formed House of Warburg, and the key that opened the door to advancement was called Rothschild.

The chief need of the freed city was to replenish its depleted stock of silver currency, and it was in this connection that letters from M. M. Warburg and Sons were sent to N. M. Rothschild and Sons in London, assuring the latter that they were capable of handling bills of exchange as speedily and effectively as any firm in Hamburg. It is the first recorded correspondence between the two firms.

THE WARBURGS

Although the Rothschild family was of more recent origin than the Warburg, at that time, and for many years to come, they were already in a different financial league.

For their part, for most of the nineteenth century the Warburgs kept their heads down and expanded slowly. In 1867, following the grant in 1849 of full citizenship to all the Jews of Hamburg, the bank's designation was changed from *Geldwechsler* to *Bankier*. But as late as 1868 M. M. Warburg & Co. as it now became had only ten employees and a messenger. Twenty years later the number of employees had increased by no more than thirteen. The firm was known as cautious and reliable, confined largely to money-changing and trade bills, carrying on a strictly orthodox banking business with no frills.

However, one member of the family was associated with a flamboyant financial maneuver. In 1857 a worldwide commodity crisis was precipitated by the failure of 150 banks in the United States. It spread to Germany and particularly to Hamburg, where bankers had issued and accepted a disproportionate number of trade bills not covered by commodity transactions. There was urgent need for a loan of 10 million marks. Prussia refused, and Austria was approached. Paul Schiff, the head of Austria's leading bank, the Kreditanstalt, was married to a Warburg daughter. For whatever reason, he decided to save Hamburg's financial reputation. He brought pressure to bear on the Austrian finance minister, who in turn approached Emperor Franz Joseph. Off from Vienna, on the emperor's orders, went a special train loaded with silver ingots. It remained for six months, untouched, in a Hamburg siding, and was then returned plus interest to Vienna. Its very existence had been enough to solve the crisis of confidence. The fame that accrued to Schiff from this operation rubbed off, through his wife, onto the Warburgs. It gave them a new stature in a grateful Hamburg.

This would not be the only occasion on which the Warburg cause benefited from a foreign marriage. It has been said of the

Hapsburg dynasty: *Bella gerunt alii, sed tu felix Austria nube* ("Others may wage war, but you, happy Austria, just marry"). This phrase might equally apply to the Warburg family.

Another instance, with a slightly comic denouement, involved the Russian banking family of Von Günzberg. Baron Alexandre, like Paul Schiff, had married a Warburg. Prior to this marriage his firm had become overinvolved in the development of the Lena goldfields recently discovered in Western Siberia. M. M. Warburg & Co., together with other firms, came to the rescue with seven million marks.

Sometime later the baron was able to repay the entire loan with interest. He did so in flamboyant fashion. At a banquet at Saint Petersburg given for his creditors, including several members of the Warburg family, he announced, "Under your plates you will find gold coins in full repayment of my indebtedness to you. Behind your seats you will find leather bags to put them into. They will enable you to enjoy your dinner more."

But the real progress of M. M. Warburg & Co. during the middle years of the nineteenth century is best illustrated by their participation, through the good offices of the Rothschild firm, in the French loan that Rothschilds issued for the payment of reparations imposed on her by Bismarck after the Franco-Prussian War of 1870–71. This, according to Edward Rosenbaum, was a landmark "in the international movement of merchandise, precious metals, commercial and financial bills and all sorts of foreign investments." [4]

That Warburgs were a part of this operation demonstrated their position among the leading and best-known dealers in the foreign exchange market. The history of the family fortune had been a case, so far, of "hastening slowly"—but to excellent purpose—and always they were amassing wealth.

[4] Edward Rosenbaum, "M. M. Warburg and Co., Merchant Bankers of Hamburg," in *Year Book VII* (New York: Leo Baeck Institute of Jews from Germany 1963).

THE WARBURGS

During this period the head of Warburgs was Abraham (Aby Samuel). After his death in 1856 his sons Siegmund and Moritz assumed titular leadership. But the real power lay with Aby Samuel's wife Sara. Sara was a formidable matriarch.

Even while her husband was alive she got her own way. Every summer they rented a house—always the same house—nearer the twin Alster lakes, but only a short distance from their winter home on Hamburg's Rothenbaumchaussee. One winter day Sara said to Aby, "Don't forget to rent the summer house again."

"Of course."

Later she asked, "Have you rented it?"

Aby had forgotten but lied and said he had. Then he discovered that someone else had rented it. In despair he approached the nineteenth-century equivalent of a real-estate agent. "What can I do?"

What could he do? Buy the house—naturally, for a very large sum—and in this way (by Hamburg law) cancel the previous tenancy.

In the end Sara, of course, discovered both his lie and his evasive extravagance; but like the shrewd woman she was she "forgave" him, for after all, the summer house had been preserved.

By the 1840s the Warburg wealth was considerable, according to the unpublished reminiscences of Sara's daughter-in-law Charlotte. Though a daughter of the wealthy Oppenheim family of Frankfurt am Main, she was astonished by the glitter and luxury of the new home Sara had prepared for her at Grindelhof, overlooking "the Moowreide, a large pasture where cattle used to graze." (Later they moved to the more fashionable Mittelweg.)

One evening in July, 1864, I arrived in Hamburg, which was to be my new home. On my arrival the house at Grindelhof was all illuminated and decorated with many-colored flags.

When we were shown around the elegant and stylish rooms on the ground floor and the cozy ones on the first floor and when finally I met the pretty cook and the maid in the brightly lit kitchen which was spick and span—I was at a loss for words. This big house with its many rooms was meant for us all alone! . . . The house was beautiful indeed. On the ground floor there was a large dining room with a pantry and, adjacent to that, a drawing room with red damask furniture and another small Turkish-styled drawing room. Marianne and Malchen [her sisters-in-law] had embroidered the coverings for the latter.

On the first floor there was a cozy living room with brown rep furniture. Near the window stood a completely equipped sewing table, a bookcase and a little piano. Next to this room was the breakfast room, its main attraction for me being an old-fashioned bureau which had belonged to mother's mother.

When I opened the flap I found a little "account book," stationery of all kinds, ink, pens—in short there was nothing missing. There was also a little pigeonhole for the household cash box.

Moreover, this room accommodated a cupboard for the tea things. This was something new to me. Here I found cups, saucers, two brass tins, one each for coffee and sugar, a teapot, etc. I was told that a proper Hamburg housewife would prepare tea and coffee in this breakfast room and would do the dishes herself following breakfast and put all the things back into this cupboard.

In addition the first floor accommodated the bedroom decorated in gray cretonne with rose designs. Next to this was a room crowded with mahogany cupboards which in turn led to the exceptionally pretty bathroom. Our own bathroom. I would never have dreamt of such a thing in our home in Frankfurt.

On the second floor were the attic and guest room.

The location of the house was very nice. At one side there was a garden and opposite there were small houses. The sight of the Hamburg maids dressed in brightly colored cotton dresses, white aprons and white caps with tulle ribbons was a perfect delight for me. From morning to night they looked neatly dressed, which was a great contrast to the more casually dressed maids of southern Germany.

Charlotte characterizes her formidable mother-in-law:

She was very particular about outward appearance and would often say, "The older one gets the more importance one should attach to one's outward appearance." She ruled her house with a stern hand. She was very kind to her subordinates. However, they had to obey. . . . She was sincerely and deeply religious and rigidly observed all customs prevailing in our religion and did all in her power to make her children cling to them, and they lived their lives just as she expected them to do it. She paid attention to a certain amount of etiquette, i.e., the way she expected her children to deal with her. She always held that certain barriers were necessary and that they did not impair love. She insisted on sons and daughters-in-law addressing her with *Sie*.[5]

After her husband's death Sara in effect took sole control of the firm. Her right-hand man was Warburgs' longtime manager, Herr Dorner. Her two sons were young and inexperienced. It has been suggested that she made certain they should remain so. It is a moot point whether in her lifetime Siegmund or Moritz—or, indeed, their father—can have lived very happy lives.

The sons' regime was strict, their hours intolerably long. Each day after the Hamburg Stock Exchange closed, the two brothers had to bring their account books for their mother's inspection and were then thoroughly grilled on the day's activities.

Certainly it was Sara who masterminded the successful Warburg participation in the French "reparations" loan of 1871.

Sara moved not only in the Hamburg society of merchants, shipowners, and bankers but also numbered among her friends, outside the free port, many artists and writers, including the poet Heinrich Heine. For many years she was a correspondent and friend, at one remove, of the first chancellor of the new German Empire, Prince Otto von Bismarck. The intermediary was a stockbroker by the name of Vogt. The quality of this relationship is made clear by a family anecdote. Bismarck was inordinately fond of rich food. Each year at the Jewish Passover (and the Gentile Easter) Sara would send him the special, and rich, Portuguese-Jewish butter cake. Then there was appointed as court chaplain to the king of Prussia a virulent anti-Jewish preacher. Bismarck had nothing to do with the appointment, but he ceased to receive the butter cake. He

[5] Instead of the more intimate *Du*.

complained to Vogt, the intermediary. The complaint was passed on. Sara replied adamantly, "If he thinks hard enough, he will know."

Sara Warburg lived until 1884. In the words of her grandson Max, "She had lived with her God." It is entirely possible she regarded God as something of an equal.

It was during the "triumvirate" of Sara, Siegmund, and Moritz that the Warburgs really took their place on the stage of international banking. From the modest beginnings of a bill-broker there now emerged a merchant banker.

But what exactly *is* a merchant banker, as opposed to a mere bill-broker, or money-lender? According to the present Sir Siegmund Warburg, a merchant banker is the "family doctor of finance." His London based firm, S. G. Warburg and Co., like Kuhn, Loeb in New York and Warburgs' in Hamburg, advises both individuals and companies on investments. Often this function involves active participation by the banks themselves; that is, the bank risks the funds of its owners. In times of financial disorder, this risk-taking makes the merchant banks extremely vulnerable.

The Encyclopaedia Brittanica puts it this way: "Merchant bankers are a special class of bankers. They do not depend mainly on deposits, like an ordinary bank, but use their capital and the power of their credit to carry on certain classes of business involving the movement of large sums and remunerated by commission. Issuing [or merchant] banks act as intermediaries between the company promoters or public authorities who seek to raise capital and the investment which provides it."

Though it was not until the mid-nineteenth century that in Germany the Warburgs were allowed to call themselves "bankiers," they had all along been using their own funds to finance new enterprises. For as one merchant banker pithily put it: a merchant banker is only a moneylender become respectable, and the Warburgs had been lending money for almost two centuries.

❧ CHAPTER TWO

The Growth of
the Family

THERE hangs today in the big house at Kösterberg, on the outskirts of Hamburg (now owned by Eric, the present head of Warburgs'), a portrait of Moritz and Charlotte in old age. They sit at a big bay window looking down over the Elbe. He is contemplative, content; she, in white lace cap, is busily writing. She seems the more active personality, and to judge from correspondence and reminiscences, in family affairs she probably was. Her granddaughter, Lola Hahn Warburg, describes her as having

an outlook on mankind decided by no whims, disciplined, measuring each emotion. I remember no superlatives in her speech. [In her old age] she was always to be found at her writing table, listening and interpreting so that later in simple language she could give her beloved children in America a picture of her life. . . . Praise from grandmother we valued above everything else.

Charlotte was a member of the Oppenheim family, diamond merchants of Frankfurt am Main. When she married Moritz, the Frankfurt ghetto was a comparatively recent memory for her and her family. It is not surprising that there was more iron in her makeup than in that of her mother-ridden husband.

As in Victorian England, children in Hamburg were kept mainly out of sight. Although Charlotte adored hers, she left them almost entirely in the care of a governess, in obedience to convention.

Hamburg in the late nineteenth century resembled the England of Victoria in more than one respect. Charlotte's new house had a Victorian Gothic porch, and there was the custom of afternoon tea. As in England an hour with mother in the early evening was the children's normal ration for the day. Though she certainly was fond of her five sons and two daughters, if one of them sat down on a chair unbidden she was apt to bark, "Don't spoil the furniture." She was a stern, meticulous housekeeper who, in the words of another daughter, "locked up the last coffee bean," but she could not cook. She had that genuine love of music that had already been evidenced in the Warburg story by the Danish Pius and was to persist in a subsequent generation. Before her marriage her proudest boast was that she had had several articles accepted in a Frankfurt magazine. She was in fact a bluestocking *manquée.*

Moritz, born in 1838, remains a more shadowy figure. As a youth he was apprenticed to the Rothschilds in Paris and later in Italy. His letters to his mother Sara display the naiveté produced by a cloistered childhood. He was wide-eyed about girls, amazed at the beauties of nature, and developing a love of pictures. He liked to speculate, from little experience, about the nature of people. If the letters paint an engaging self-portrait they do not conceal the very strict and orthodox Jew. For example, a repetitive feature of his letters home are descriptions of his search for kosher restaurants —often very *long* searches.

Yet this pious young man was to develop into one of the most highly respected bankers of his day. At the beginning of his banking career he pursued a line of strict caution, and to the end this was his chosen way. His favorite Shakespearean quotation was *Der guter Name ist das eisentliches kleinod* ("A good name is the true jewel"). It was that good name that was the springboard for the leap forward engineered by his son Max around the turn of the century that brought Warburgs into the very front rank of merchant bankers. Between 1891 and 1910 (the year Moritz died) the firm's turnover increased sixfold.

During Moritz's day the offices, his son Max recalls in his memoirs, were small and primitive by Hamburg standards, lit only by oil lamps and very dark. They were dominated by a very large green sofa, which had been lent ten years before by Moritz himself. On one occasion Max woke his father, who, unbuttoned, was sleeping on it, with the news, "Baron Rothschild is here." Brother of the great Alphonse, the baron had arrived in Hamburg on his famous snow-white steam yacht. Moritz leaped from the sofa, his fatigue transformed to warm welcome. Paying attention to the Rothschilds was not only a habit but good business. One wonders which of the three wigs he wore regularly to hide his baldness Moritz donned on this occasion.

Max wrote of his father:

Lovable, hard-working, gifted with diplomatic talents, Moritz gave the firm a reputation well ahead of its actual performance. He was concerned more with the good name of the firm than financial gain and he refused many profitable transactions which he thought unworthy. The following generation owed much to him, and his motto of *Labor et Constantia*.[1]

In the peroration at Moritz's funeral the presiding rabbi referred to the impressions of ancient Jewish piety that Moritz had inherited from his mother Sara:

In his youth his intoxicated eyes had soaked up Judaism; his years of manhood enclosed and embraced it with powerful arms never to abandon it. To his old age it was the staff on which, undaunted, he liked to lean toward the melancholy going down of the sun. It fulfilled in him the sense of those great words which are read on the Sabbath in Israel's godly temples and which shall become for him the great Sabbath of liberation.

[1] Memoirs of Max Warburg, 1952, Hamburg, Germany.

Hyperbole at funerals is common to clergymen of all denominations. It is, indeed, demanded of them by their congregations. Certainly the rabbi was no exception to this rule, but his effusiveness underlined an important truth: Moritz Warburg ended as he began, a Jew of the strictest orthodoxy.

For many years he had been the official leader of Hamburg's Jewish community. He was the leading spirit in the administration of the Israeli Orphanage and for thirty years supervised the activities of the Talmud Torah *Realschule*. In both time and money he gave generously to the propagation of Judaism in all its observances.

"His great love of Judaism grew and flourished in the depths of his soul," the rabbi had said at his funeral. Moritz, Charlotte, and Moritz's mother were Jewish first and German second.

Between 1866 and 1879 Charlotte Warburg bore her husband five sons. Aby was the firstborn in 1860, Max was born in 1867, Paul in 1868, Felix in 1871, and Fritz in 1879. Widely differing in their temperaments and activities, they led the Warburg family into the modern world and are known today among their descendants as the "Famous Five." [2]

The children were brought up by a devoted mother who because of the custom of the time left them largely in the hands of their outstanding governess. They lived in Hamburg in bourgeois comfort and seldom traveled farther than Frankfurt. Both parents demanded stringent obedience to the strictest tenets of orthodox Judaism. The rabbi's word must be law. He had their education in his hands. But from the day the Jews of Germany were granted full citizenship the world around them had begun to change: Contact with the Gentile world became possible for both business and social ends. Yet the orthodox Jew still voluntarily denied himself these opportunities.

To a greater or lesser extent all Moritz's offspring, despite their

[2] In the author's view, they should be the "Famous Four." Fritz was hardly of the caliber of his brothers. There were also two daughters.

orthodox upbringing, sought accommodation with the world around them, in Germany and later in the United States. The dark clouds of oppression, which had so long hung over the Jewish race, were lifting in Western Europe and America. Perhaps Moritz and Charlotte never realized this, but subconsciously even as very young men their sons did. Their parents' insistence on Judaism in all its forms—the strict observance of the Sabbath, the avoidance of Gentile contacts, the eating only at kosher restaurants—drove them into rebellion, toward what they imagined was the full sunlight of a rapidly changing world.

Reform might well have been in the air. Nevertheless, as children their futures seemed predestined. As with most middle-class English or American families at that time, the parents chose their careers. By custom Aby, the eldest, would succeed his father as head of the bank, and Max and Paul, the next two in seniority, would become partners. Felix would be apprenticed to his mother's family of diamond merchants, and Fritz would become a lawyer. Though Felix was destined for other things, he did learn one maxim and one mannerism from his brief apprenticeship with his Oppenheim grandfather. The maxim was: "To sell a man pearls that you have got and that he wants, that is not business. To sell a man pearls that you have not got and that he does not want, that is business." The mannerism was a lifelong habit of sitting with his arms folded across his chest. His grandfather advised this as a precaution against going to sleep in a railway carriage and having the bag of diamonds he would be carrying stolen while he slept.

So there they were: three bankers, a diamond broker, a lawyer in embryo.

Aby, the firstborn, also was the first to break the pattern. He wanted to study art and become an art historian. According to Warburg tradition, while still a very young adolescent he went to his brother Max, one year his junior, and said, "You can have any position in the bank, provided you'll always pay for any book I want to buy." Max gleefully accepted.

A less dramatic version is given by E. H. Gombrich, head of the Warburg Institute in London, in his recently published life of Aby Warburg. According to Professor Gombrich, Aby went not to his brother but to his father and told him of his desire. His father somewhat reluctantly assented and promised initial financial help, which through the years the family continued.[3] But Max in his own memoirs gives a third version:

> When I was twelve years old Aby put to me the proposal that I should buy from him his birthright, not indeed for a mess of pottage but against my pledge that I would always pay for his book purchases. I was a child, and the bargain seemed to me splendid. I would certainly now inherit my father's business at the price of having to buy Schiller, Goethe and perhaps Klopstock. We sealed this pact happily with a handshake. This agreement was the most light-hearted of my life. But truly I have never regretted it.[4]

Moritz on the other hand probably did think his eldest son had sold his birthright for a mess of pottage. Art historian, books—the family firm was worth a lot more than that!

Max, then, would be the next head of M. M. Warburg & Co., and Paul his younger brother would be his right-hand man. For the moment Felix still seemed fated, by parental decision, to be a diamond broker.

Max was twenty-seven, Paul was twenty-six, and Felix twenty-three, when in 1894 Jacob Schiff, with his wife and daughter, paid a visit to Frankfurt. Felix was working in the Oppenheim business, and Moritz and Charlotte were by chance paying him a visit.

[3] E. H. Gombrich, *Aby M. Warburg* (London, 1970).

[4] Memoirs of Max Warburg, 1952, Hamburg, Germany.

CHAPTER THREE

Enter Jacob Schiff

In 1894, at the age of forty-seven, Jacob Schiff was probably the most famous Jew in New York. He was certainly one of the richest men in America.

He came from an ancient lineage—the Warburg family tree, started in the 1500s, is modest by comparison. The Schiff tree goes back in detail to the fourteenth century, and the family even used to claim King Solomon as an ancestor.

In the early nineteenth century the family shared a house in the Judengasse in Frankfurt with what seemed to them the parvenu, because so much more recent in origin, Rothschilds.

Jacob's father was a successful stockbroker, but Jacob even as a very young man was restless. At the age of eighteen, after careful plotting, he departed, unknown to his parents, for America.

His first venture there—a brokerage business—petered out. Momentarily disheartened, he returned to Germany and became manager of the Deutsche Bank in Hamburg. There he met the Warburg family for the first time, Moritz and Charlotte and their small children. He gave the boys a toy fort. There also he met Abraham Kuhn, who had retired from the firm of Kuhn, Loeb, which he had helped to found in New York. Abraham advised him to write to his ex-partner, Solomon Loeb. Jacob did so, and in 1873 returned to New York and joined the firm. Casting aside earlier setbacks, he rose meteorically. By 1875 he was a full partner.

In the next twenty years Jacob Schiff, by a mixture of shrewd-ness, hard work, and sheer financial wizardry, made a fortune, mainly out of railways, for his firm and for himself. When he visited Frankfurt in 1894, he was certainly a dollar millionaire. He had also married Solomon Loeb's eldest daughter and had pushed his father-in-law and original benefactor almost completely into the background. Kuhn, Loeb was now synonymous with Schiff.

Frieda Schiff was her father's only daughter. He adored her, but it was the adoration of a strict, straitlaced family autocrat who did not hesitate to discipline his children—even in public.

On one occasion he paid a visit to his son Mortimer (Morti), who was apprenticed to the merchant banking firm of Samuel Montagu in London. At a large reception Morti appeared in a lavender-gray suit, which according to Jacob Schiff clashed with his yellow topcoat. In front of the assembled company Jacob ordered him home to change his clothes.

But Morti, at least for business purposes, was allowed to travel on his own. Frieda was never allowed out from under her parents' wings. At the age of eighteen she knew nothing of the world outside her own family and its retainers. Whenever she went out she was heavily chaperoned; she must not be allowed to do anything, to go anywhere, unprotected. She knew little about men and nothing about the facts of life.

It cannot have been an easy upbringing, for Jacob Schiff, though he could be a genial, loving paterfamilias, was also subject at the most unexpected moments to violent outbreaks of ungovernable temper. Pretty, lively when it was permissible, and surrounded by the rich things of life, Frieda was in many ways a poor little rich girl.

In that summer of 1894, forewarned of the Schiffs' arrival in Frankfurt, some cousins of the Schiff family arranged a dinner dance in Frieda's honor. In view of Jacob's friendship with the Warburgs in Hamburg twenty years earlier, it was natural that Moritz and Charlotte and their children should be invited. Felix,

Frieda was warned, was something of a ladies' man—handsome, and with a reputation for wit. She looked forward to meeting him.

On the other hand, when the Schiffs arrived in Frankfurt he was in London and might not be back in time. But by the evening of the party he was there and placed next to her at the dinner table. She was delighted with him. He exceeded the fondest expectations of this totally unsophisticated girl.

And Felix? He was more than delighted, he was in love. Bursting into his parents' bedroom long after midnight, he exclaimed, "I have met the girl I am going to marry."

Yet time was to pass, and many maneuvers, before he asked her. Both sets of parents were horrified by the thought, failing to notice that Frieda, as she makes clear in her unpublished memoirs, did not yet know Felix's plan.

Moritz and Charlotte—particularly Moritz—hated the thought that Felix might have to live in America. An official leader of Hamburg's Jews, Moritz strongly opposed the waves of Jewish emigrants from Germany to the United States that had started in the 1850s and increased each succeeding decade. Primarily, the emigration was due to the lure of the new Promised Land, but a secondary reason for some was probably the initially mild but insidious growth in Germany of anti-Semitism, one result of Jews' becoming partially assimilated into German life.

Moritz had another more personal reason for not wanting his son to live in America. He had a morbid fear of crossing the Atlantic. "The sea is not solid," he would exclaim.

As for Jacob Schiff, he raged and fumed for a number of reasons. In his calmer moments he admitted that the Warburgs were good solid stock, of fairly ancient lineage, but in the world of high finance or of personal wealth they were at that time hardly in his league. About one thing Jacob was determined: His daughter would never live in Germany. Like practically every other Jew who had emigrated to the United States and made his fortune there, he had resolutely turned his back on his native country. Above all, how could he contemplate that his daughter at the age of eighteen should marry, and to a young man with a reputation as "flashy" as Felix's?

The morning after Felix's startling pronouncement the Warburgs called on the Schiffs. The meeting was frigid and inconclusive, and the Schiffs soon left for Paris. At the Longchamps races Felix, uninvited, joined them.

Frieda was shipped off to London, where she immediately fell ill, and the benign figure of Sir Ernest Cassel entered the drama. He and Jacob had for years been close business associates, Sir Ernest being in fact if not in name Kuhn, Loeb's chief adviser on European matters. Surprisingly, they had become personal friends as well.

There seemed little in common between the stark and intensely religious Schiff and the genial man of the world who had totally abandoned his Jewish faith and was a friend and financial adviser to the raffish Prince of Wales and the Marlborough House set. Yet according to Frieda each man vied to give the other the more valuable birthday present.

Sir Ernest chaperoned Frieda in London and perhaps managed to educate her a little as well.

Frieda's sojourn in London, after her parents and brother Morti had joined her, was followed by a Scandinavian cruise and a brief visit to the Warburgs in Hamburg. (Felix was safely in Frankfurt.)

For the first time Frieda met Felix's brother Max, and in her own words, "the charm of the Warburgs was deeply impressed upon me." Then Jacob (and his family) took the cure at Bad Gastein.

Here Felix reappeared. One day the couple managed to evade the attentions of every Schiff in sight, and Felix took Frieda for a walk. Felix asked her whether she would like to spend her life in Germany. When she rejoined her mother she exclaimed, "I think that fellow proposed."

The moment of crisis had been reached, for Frieda left her mother in no doubt that she was in love. That evening Sir Ernest Cassel gave a dinner party for the Schiffs at which Felix was present.

The atmosphere was somber. The next morning Mrs. Schiff in great agitation broke to Jacob the news of Felix's "proposal" and of the state of Frieda's emotions. He exploded.

Again Sir Ernest was at hand, assuming the mantle of Frieda's champion, to persuade the irate parent that marriage to a Warburg would not be the end of the world. Reluctantly, Jacob agreed to a joint family meeting to discuss the future. It took place at Ostend, over two formal luncheons, at one of which Jacob was made furious by the appearance of non-kosher lobster. Despite this farcical interlude he agreed that Felix and Frieda should consider themselves formally engaged.

Sir Ernest was absent from these luncheons. He had done his bit. No doubt concerned only for the happiness of two people, he had played his part nonetheless in introducing the Warburg family to a totally new and far wider field of opportunity.

Felix had won the right to woo Frieda. But he was forbidden to be ardent in his courtship. It was to be a wooing by intermediaries. Jacob insisted that there should be no direct communication between Felix and Frieda. Once a week Felix would write to Frieda a long letter which she had to read to her father. Once a week Frieda would write to Felix, Jacob reading the letter before mailing it.

Jacob insisted, too, that if the marriage did take place, Felix must abandon his career in Germany, settle in the United States, and join the firm of Kuhn, Loeb. Moritz, the junior and somewhat overawed partner in these matters, had to agree. Should he wish to visit his son, he would have to brave that wobbly Atlantic Ocean.

The arrangement lasted six months. In March, 1895, the wedding took place in New York.

It was a rich and formal affair. One hundred and forty-five guests were invited to the Schiff mansion at 932 Fifth Avenue. There was only one problem: The caterers announced that the available space would accommodate only 125. But it turned out all right in the end. A week before the wedding Mrs. James Seligman died, and her family party of precisely twenty persons had to make their excuses.

The bride wore heavy slippered satin with "yards and yards of Brussels lace." It was, Frieda records, "really too heavy for a girl of eighteen."

The wedding had a postscript as important to the Warburg family as the actual event. Felix's brother Paul crossed the Atlantic to be best man. The maid of honor was Nina Loeb, the considerably younger sister of Frieda's mother.

It was a match in the making, and within a year Paul and Nina had married.

In her brilliant record parodying the story of Wagner's *Das Ring der Niebelungen*, the British singer Anna Russell refers to Brunhilde as "the only woman Siegfried had ever met who wasn't his aunt." Paul Warburg did the neat trick of turning his brother's aunt into a sister-in-law.

CHAPTER FOUR

Max: The Rise of a Banker *1892–1914*

THE Warburg ways had divided, and the carefully laid plans of Moritz and Charlotte for their male offspring had been upset, first by the determination of a thirteen-year-old, then by the impetuous wooing of their fourth son and the rapid transformation of his brother and best man into another bridegroom. The main beneficiary of these events, as far as the firm of M. M. Warburg & Co. was concerned, was Max, who remained behind in Hamburg.

It has been said that to understand Max Warburg you must first understand Hamburg. The city and all it stood for were in his bones. This great seaport had a long and proud tradition as a member of the Hanseatic League. When in the 1820s a German customs union was formed under the leadership of Prussia, Hamburg remained aloof. She did not join it until after the creation of the German Empire in 1871, and then only in part—much of the coastal city, as opposed to its hinterland, remained outside the union.

Situated at the mouth of one of Germany's greatest rivers, the Elbe, Hamburg was the natural outlet for the great German industrial centers that sprang up in the latter half of the nineteenth century—Berlin, Magdeburg, Saxony, Bohemia, and cities farther east.

Her links with Britain, that "nation of shopkeepers" with the greatest merchant fleet in the world, had always been close, provoking Napoleon to remark that Hamburg was "a colony of England." Though in the nineteenth century these links were somewhat weakened, as late as 1869, 60 percent of the tonnage entering the port was British. In 1907 British imports through Hamburg were worth 635 million marks, half the value of all imports from the whole of continental Europe.

Hamburg was in fact Germany's open window on the world, and before World War I the Hamburg merchant and businessman moved just as easily between Hamburg and London as between Hamburg and Berlin. Even his contacts with the United States grew closer than those with the industrialists of Germany. He looked out through his open window, but he resented anyone who tried to peer through it—a competitor, a cartel, above all the State.

In the days when Max was growing up, this beautiful, spacious city exuded a spirit of enterprise. The winds of the world blew along the wide reaches of the River Elbe and penetrated to the twin lakes, the greater and lesser Alster, that dominated its center.

It was a city totally committed to business activities, and culturally a desert—even lacking a university of any sort. It matched to perfection and did much to mold the extroverted, optimistic young banker who took actual control of M. M. Warburg & Co. in the early years of the twentieth century. One of Max's closest friends was Albert Ballin, the Jew who rose from nothing to become head of the Hamburg-Amerika shipping line (HAPAG), by 1900 the largest steamship line in the world.

But Max had also had his moment of rebellion. As a youth he was conscripted into the army. He liked army life so much he told his father he would like to make it his profession. At the time Jews were never allowed to become commissioned officers, and Moritz prudently vetoed the suggestion; he himself had been forced to be content to serve as a lowly trumpeter.

In 1890 Max was sent by his father as an apprentice to the Imperial Ottoman Bank of Paris. It was his first time abroad. There he combined work and pleasure in about equal proportions. He kept two establishments—one on the fashionable Right Bank; another, more free and easy, in the Latin Quarter.

He even attended the Sorbonne with the idea of taking his doctorate, but this remained only a notion.

"It was a turbulent, marvelously exciting time and of course of great value to me. I learned much about the land, the people, and about life." [1]

At one stage he appears to have engaged in a mild form of bribery—of course on the orders of his superiors. The Ottoman Bank had agreed to sponsor the conversion of a Turkish loan. Favorable coverage by the press could be a valuable asset in the operation. Max sat at the bank's counter, empowered to hand to any owner of a newspaper who asked for it a check made out to an amount agreed upon with an important representative of the daily press. One day a gentleman appeared and asked for the thousand-franc check that had been reserved for him. When Max paused momentarily to consult his records, the visitor exclaimed indignantly, "You ignore the importance of my newspaper."

"But I read it every day."

"My newspaper only appears weekly."

Max does not record whether he handed over the check.

From Paris Max moved to London, where he continued his apprenticeship in the House of Rothschild at their city offices, Number 1, New Court.

Initially, London seemed stuffy to Max. The flowery cravats and bare head of his Paris days had to be replaced by a bowler hat, sober suit, and unobtrusive shirt. *Le phlegme anglais* had at least to be simulated.

As compensation he was not required to overwork. At first he arrived at New Court punctually at 9:00 A.M. each morning and joined the other juniors in opening the mail. Very soon, however,

[1] Memoirs of Max Warburg, 1952, Hamburg, Germany.

the then Lord Rothschild told him sternly, "A perfect gentleman never comes to the office before ten o'clock in the morning. Or," he added, "stays after four in the afternoon." [2]

The reasoning behind the ban on an early arrival for Max was not based entirely on an aristocratic disdain for looking as though he were trying too hard. If this particular young gentleman started opening the mail he might get to know too much; after all, he did come from a rival business.

Again in his own words, Max "came to love this land and its people." [3] He never lost that love. It was an emotion not difficult to sustain for a citizen of Hamburg, with its centuries-long tradition of friendship across the North Sea.

In 1892 his father summoned him back to Hamburg. The apprenticeship was over—and so was the time for playing society's games. Once again Max disliked the move. Paris and London had offered him much, and with his gaiety, quick mind, and gift for friendship he had had no difficulty in grasping what was offered. Though on his return he was appointed only as *Prokurist* ("confidential clerk"), all concerned knew that in effect, after a brief schooling, he would control the firm. Moritz still had eighteen years to live, but the cares of the bank—perhaps above all its rapid expansion—had weighed heavily upon him. The portrait of him and Charlotte shows him pensive and relaxed. His son made this quiet ending possible.

Max became a *Teilhaber* ("full partner") in Warburgs a year later, and in that same year (1893) his brother Paul (one year his junior) joined the firm as *Prokurist*. In 1895 Paul also became a full partner, but a few months later, as we have seen, he married Nina Loeb.

[2] Ten to four—what Lord Rothschild preached in 1891, the British trade unions are preaching eighty years later in their search for a three-day week. In contrast, British bankers today work longer hours than their equivalents in any other country, and the City of London remains, however shakily, the financial center of the world.

[3] Memoirs of Max Warburg.

THE WARBURGS

It is interesting to speculate what would have happened, if in the years to follow, these two brothers, so different in temperament, so comparable in intellectual ability, had worked in daily contact with each other. Would the bank have taken more effective steps to cushion the impact of war? Would it have fared differently in the financial crises that hit it in 1923 and 1931? Or would these crises never have occurred, because the rapid expansion of the firm's fortunes in the early years of Max's stewardship would have been braked by his brother's far less sunny outlook? No one can tell, because though Paul Warburg remained a partner in M. M. Warburg until 1907, and a reasonably active partner until 1902, in the latter year he was made a partner in Kuhn, Loeb, and at the demand, thinly disguised as a request, of his formidable brother-in-law, Jacob Schiff, took up permanent residence in America. Even before 1902 he was only a commuting partner, half his time being spent in New York.

His son, James P. (Jimmy) Warburg, has described the cavalcade that set forth each year to cross the Atlantic:

We traveled with a valet-butler and lady's maid, as well as a nurse or governess. Wilhelm Toerber, the valet-butler, took charge of the baggage, which consisted of a number of large trunks for the ship's hold, hatboxes, blanket-rolls, "steamer trunks," and innumerable suitcases and valises to be stowed in the cabins. The cook and one or two maids traveled on a separate ship.[4]

The Warburgs were becoming very rich. They were becoming internationally famous, too. Jimmy records his child's-eye view of the establishment at Kösterberg:

Diplomats, bankers and businessmen from other countries visited M. M. Warburg & Co., and not infrequently came to Kösterberg. One night, when the Russian Consul-General was having dinner with my parents and several other guests on the verandah I was asked to fetch his hat, because a cold wind was blowing. When I returned with the right hat my proud

[4] James P. Warburg, *The Long Road Home* (New York, 1964), p. 15.

father asked me how I had been able to identify it. To his horror I replied, "By the funny smell."

Besides Paul the partners in Warburgs included Max's cousin Aby S. Warburg, and after 1907 his youngest brother Fritz. Fritz was to play an important part in developing the private-client side of the business—one client was Marcel Proust. He also reorganized and rebuilt the old bank premises on Ferdinandstrasse to cope with the very large flow of additional business that Max was generating and that now required a staff not of ten but of well over a hundred.

Aby S. Warburg was in the older tradition of Moritz, a cautious and sound banker, but it was Max who, in fact if not in name, made all the important decisions. Fritz later paid his older brother an indirect tribute made more eloquent by Max's tendency to treat him, his junior by twelve years, with condescension.

"In retrospect one might say," Fritz wrote, "that the years from 1900 to 1914 were the years of the most happy and harmonious development of the firm."

The groundwork for this growth had been laid in the 1890s. Max had returned to Hamburg in 1892. He at once became active in the city's civic affairs and accepted several honorary posts. It was a rapid and complete switch from the near playboy role of his Paris and London apprenticeships.

In 1897 he became a Commercial Judge. In 1902 he was elected to the Hamburg Chamber of Commerce, and in 1903 to the Hamburg State Parliament. Both posts were useful adjuncts to his career as a merchant banker. At the end of 1898 (the hundredth anniversary of the firm's founding) Max became engaged to Alice Magnus, whose family was related to the Altona Warburgs. "It was," Max reflected many years later, "an eventful year for my friends and myself. Betrothals and weddings of brothers and sisters followed fast one after the other."

Two years earlier his father had at last been persuaded to buy the estate of Kösterberg, which Max had long coveted as the most beautifully situated property within reach of Hamburg. Here he and his parents added new houses for older relatives and brothers and sisters, constructed hothouses, a swimming pool, and a tennis court. They gave it all the trappings of unostentatious wealth. They loved it dearly.

Such was Max's happy family life. But business opportunities beckoned. The nineteenth century was, among other things, the age of industrialization. Britain led the way, but by the end of the century she was being rivaled, if not outstripped, by Germany and the United States. Others, most importantly Japan, joined the race a little later but soon caught up. Inevitably this worldwide industrialization resulted in a great expansion of international trade, which in turn created a massive demand for loans to finance it. Loans, or "risk capital," were what merchant bankers such as M. M. Warburg & Sons were all about.

To take risks was second nature to Max, and in those halcyon years that preceded the outbreak of World War I it looked as though he didn't know how to make a mistake. Boldness and initiative were the order of the day, and Max was the man to display them.

In his and the firm's rapid upward climb, Max owed much to his close friend, Albert Ballin. Ballin was a self-made Hamburg Jew whose father had bankrupted the family business. Ballin had then built up almost single-handedly the Hamburg-Amerika Line (HA-PAG), which in the early years of this century rivaled the British Cunard Shipping Company as the most successful carrier in the North Atlantic shipping lanes. In the words of his biographer Lamarr Cecil:

> Ballin's most intimate friend ... was Max M. Warburg, the senior partner of his family's famous banking house in Hamburg. The two men were virtually in a state of continuous communication, by letter, by conference, and by a private telephone line, which ran between their neighboring office buildings.[5]

[5] Lamarr Cecil, *Ballin* (New York, 1967), p. 136.

Ballin was accepted and respected in the world of big business, he had the ear of the politicians, and he was received in court circles, becoming a close friend of the German emperor, Kaiser Wilhelm II.

He was a social as well as a business asset to Max Warburg. The list of guests in the visitors' book at his country house reads almost like the *Almanach de Gotha*. No Rothschild in Paris, Sassoon in London, Schiff or Seligman in New York could match it. In those Edwardian days the country house was often the setting for business deals, high politics, and finance. Together the two men, banker and shipowner, marched forward, expanding their influence and gaining one financial triumph after another.

Max's first really major transaction took place in 1903. With his brother Paul playing a part, he placed in the United States a loan of 80 million marks of German treasury bonds.

In this negotiation the firm of Kuhn, Loeb played no part.

In 1905 Warburgs were invited to join the *Reichsanleihe-Konzortium* ("state consortium for raising loans"), a grouping of some fifty firms of varying sizes. In the same year Max participated in the floating of a giant international Japanese loan, needed as a result of the Russo-Japanese War. As was the case with Britain after fighting victoriously in both world wars, the Japanese victory entailed severe financial penalties. This time the invitation came from Kuhn, Loeb. Paul—if not Felix—was already firmly established in the counsels of Jacob Schiff's empire. Max, when he received the invitation to contribute to the loan, "did what any trade banker would do in such circumstances. I went to the Foreign Office and consulted with Zimmermann [the under secretary]. He was taken with the idea. So I negotiated successfully with the Japanese representative in London. This was the beginning of many Japanese transactions."

Max's visit to Zimmermann also marked his entry into the political arena. He had realized that with a loan of such size and such strong international implications no banker could go it alone without seeking his ruler's consent. The Warburg participation in the Japanese loan opened up a large volume of trade with this new dynamo of the Far East to the benefit of both Warburgs and Germany. It marked, too, the beginning of Max's long friendship with the Japanese negotiator Korekejo Takahashi, who sent his daughter to be educated in America as the guest of the Jacob Schiffs.[6]

In that first decade of the twentieth century commercial expansion was in the air, and Max basked in it freely. Turnover totals rose from 10 million marks in 1892 to 105 million in 1910.

According to Edward Rosenbaum, "During this period—in spite of their growing participation in public loans—Warburgs remained the leading firm in the market of commercial bills and foreign currencies. The portfolio of commercial bills sometimes reached the amount of 50 million marks." [7]

The first fourteen years of the twentieth century proved to be the heyday of Max Warburg's career. In 1892, when he had returned to Hamburg, he was still an unknown, comparatively young man. Rapidly he became an important figure in Hamburg business circles and a growing power in international finance, with the strongest connections not only with Kuhn, Loeb but with comparable houses in Paris, London, Copenhagen, and Stockholm. There were setbacks, but he rode them out skillfully. By 1914 he was internationally famous. Never again would Max experience an era of such success.

There was only one cloud on the horizon. Certainly as early as 1907 Max was aware of the threat of war, for in that year he made a speech deploring the lack of any financial planning to meet a possible outbreak of hostilities. The ultimate disaster, he felt, would be war with England. Anglo-German rivalry, prompted by fear on the

---

[6] Takahashi later became finance minister and then premier of Japan and was murdered in 1936 at the age of eighty for his opposition to his country's militarists.
[7] M. M. Warburg & Co.

one hand and frustrated ambition on the other, might well provoke it unless some sort of agreement could be reached. Germany wanted to be a colonial power; how could she be if her access to potential colonies were frustrated by the still much stronger British fleet? How could a clash be averted?

Max was more than half in love with England, as many citizens of Hamburg had been before him. He had many friends and close contacts in the City of London, Sir Ernest Cassel chief among them. It was Max who introduced Sir Ernest to Ballin, and their growing relationship seemed for a time fruitful for peace.

Max deplored, as indeed did the German government, the Kaiser's ill-timed outburst against England in the London *Daily Telegraph* in 1908: "Like other private persons on both sides [he] was [from 1909 onward] feverishly searching for an understanding." [8] Max and Ballin were active members of the Foundation for Anglo-German Friendship launched by King Edward VII.

In the anxious days that followed the Agadir crisis of 1911 Sir Ernest Cassel chartered a 7,000-ton ship, the *Ypiranga*, of the Hamburg-Amerika Line, for an Anglo-German party of eight. The ship sailed up the coast of Norway, past Spitsbergen. The talk was all of how to avoid an Anglo-German conflict. The guests of Sir Ernest on this bizarre pleasure cruise included Colonel Wilfred Ashley, father of the future Countess Mountbatten, Ballin, and Max, with their wives.

All during this period Max was uttering warnings in high government circles, but one method of influencing events he never tried. He totally ignored democratic processes.

They were fragile enough, in all conscience, in the Germany of those days; but such as they were, he disliked them very much. Max, like Ballin, could rail against the faults, particularly of economic obscurantism, that prevailed among the Junker aristocracy that ruled the land. But he could not entertain any attempt to alter,

[8] Memoirs of Max Warburg, 1952, Hamburg, Germany.

much less to overthrow, the system, for the alternative might well be revolution. The working classes were tiresome enough as it was, with their strident demands for higher wages.

Far better the devil he knew, particularly because a man in Max's position, by his personal influence, by skillful propaganda, by the very fact of his great wealth, might well divert state policy into the paths he desired without flirting with that dangerous apparition, democracy.

As Lamarr Cecil wrote:

Men like Ballin and Warburg ... for all their technical ability and imagination, for all the critical faculties which made them aware of both the opportunities and dangers breeding in Germany's development, were not disposed to alter the world in which they lived and were unconvinced that any substantial changes were necessary.[9]

As far as politics were concerned, Max was at that time a deeply conservative man. In the opening years of the twentieth century, things in Germany were, if war could be avoided, to Max's way of thinking, very much all right. And might not even war, if it could be speedily won, be preferable to democracy?

So Max strove for peace through what were to him the normal channels, and mixed his strivings with the pursuit of business.

At the time of the Agadir crisis of 1911 his firm was guilty of an irregularity that could have caused a scandal. The German government was seeking a pretext for interfering by gunboat diplomacy in the French attempt to take over Morocco. The appearance of a German gunboat off the French-protected Moroccan port of Agadir brought Europe momentarily to the verge of war. The secretary of the German Foreign Office persuaded an employee of Warburgs to draw up a petition, to be signed by German firms carrying on business in southern Morocco, asking for protection from marauding native bands. There were no marauding natives, and the loca-

---

[9] Lamarr Cecil, *Albert Ballin* (New York, 1967), p. 141.

tions of the German concerns were well out of range of any gunboat, French or German, that anchored at Agadir. Nonetheless, a number of firms signed the petition; they included M. M. Warburg & Co.

Fortunately for Max, this incident was not publicized. There is no evidence that he knew what his employee was doing, and plenty of evidence from his character and career that he did not.

Certainly, however, he was growing increasingly interested in Morocco and other colonial operations. In his memoirs, he claims that no firm took more interest in colonial affairs, that he had helped to found the Colonial Institute in Hamburg and twice rescued the Institute of Tropical Medicine from bankruptcy. Early in 1914 he had conversations in London with Lord Milner with a view to setting up a joint Anglo-German bank in Morocco.

While the danger of war grew more apparent, the affairs of Warburgs continued to prosper. One setback, however, occurred in 1912, when the firm seemed to be heading for a loss. But it proved a case of *reculer pour mieux sauter.*

That year Max became involved, much against his will, in the affairs of Blohm and Voss, the biggest shipbuilding firm in Germany.

Two years before, this privately owned firm had been given a contract by Albert Ballin, head of the Hamburg-Amerika Line and by now Max's closest friend and business associate, to build four 20,000-ton passenger ships.

Quite soon, however, Ballin began to have doubts.

Herbert Blohm, the white-bearded, patriarchal head of the firm, might be a magnificent shipbuilder, but had he the financial resources or acumen to cope with the giant order Ballin had given him?

Wasn't Max Warburg the man to resolve Ballin's doubts? Would Max join the Blohm and Voss board?

For two years Max said no. It was highly unlikely that Herbert Blohm would welcome a financial interloper as a director of his privately owned company. Then Ballin told him that on the contrary Blohm was delighted at the thought of his joining his firm. A dinner party was arranged. Blohm expressed his pleasure at the opportunity to initiate Max into the mysteries of industrial relations and management of which, as a banker, he was naturally ignorant. It was only at that moment that Max realized the deception that Ballin had practiced. Ballin had indicated to Blohm that he was conferring a favor on Max. Blohm was to be the teacher, Max the pupil.

The deception worked. Blohm and Voss prospered. Max, the banker, whom Ballin had already made a director of HAPAG, was now intimately concerned with the biggest shipowning and shipbuilding companies in Germany. Ballin had proved to be his good angel.

In June, 1914, Max paid three visits to London. Ostensibly the reason was the proposed participation of Warburgs in a new international Brazilian loan being raised under the leadership of Rothschilds. But he also certainly urged upon his English friends the need to avoid impending disaster. Before he left for London on the first of these trips he had discussed with the German chancellor, Theobald von Bethmann-Hollweg, how war between England and Germany could be avoided. He could have had little hope, for at a dinner given for the Kaiser on June 14, 1914, at the Prussian legation in Hamburg, he besought his emperor to abandon his customary Norwegian cruise in view of the international situation.

Max had known the Kaiser since 1903. The acquaintanceship had been brought about by Ballin, who had long been the only Jew to be accepted in court circles in Berlin. Ballin arranged a meeting between the two men at a dinner in Cuxhaven. The German chancellor at the time, Prince Bernhard von Bülow, whose mother came from Hamburg, wanted Max to brief the Kaiser on financial matters.

Max's account of the interview has its farcical overtones. He would be allowed, Ballin announced, ten minutes of conversation. Max protested, and the time limit was extended, with German precision, to thirty-two minutes. In fact the conversation lasted less than the originally stipulated ten. The Kaiser would talk about nothing but Russia, which, he declared, was going broke. Max ventured to question this pronouncement, and their talk came to an abrupt end.

The next year they met again. This time the emperor was in a genial mood. Taking Max by the arm, he guided him to a big bay window and discoursed vividly on a wide variety of topics. After nearly half an hour he ended by saying, "Anyway, the Russians aren't going broke."

Without stopping to think, Max replied, "I told you that the last time."

The Kaiser thumped the table violently and shouted, "Must you always be right?" but then listened carefully to Max's views on financial matters, keenly and effectively cross-examining him.

After this meeting, though he was never among the Kaiser's intimates, Max saw him every year at the Kiel regatta, and once at a court dinner in Berlin. He came to regard him with a considerable measure of admiration. The Kaiser possessed charm, wit, and a real gift of oratory. He was deeply religious, a romantic with a flair for the arts, and very intelligent. It was his personal tragedy that no one in his family or in court circles came near to matching his intellectual gifts.

But Max realized that he lacked, for all his qualities, the stature and self-confidence to sustain his imperial role. In conversation with him Max often felt convinced that he had won agreement to his arguments, but he knew that the next man who spoke to him could easily make him change his mind.

Because the German people believed in the Kaiser's conception of himself as emperor by divine right, during World War I he had the opportunity to be a fine leader of his nation. Instead, turning his back on unselfish advisers, he allowed himself to become a figurehead for the machinations of Alfred von Tirpitz and Erich Ludendorff.

On the other hand, it would have been hard for him in those chauvinistic years 1914–18—for chauvinism is always first cousin to anti-Semitism—to make men like Ballin and Max Warburg his confidants. It might have been better for him and for his nation if he had.

In August, 1914, war broke out. Only a month before, Max had welcomed to Germany a group representing the British Adult School Organization. On its return to London the head of the group wrote on notepaper embossed with the German and British flags and a handclasp underneath, expressing their great gratitude for "the fine show of brotherly love shown to our people" and the hope that it would be possible for Max to participate in the return visit to England planned for the following year. Max received the letter four days after war had been declared.

By then, patriotic fervor had gripped the German and British peoples alike, even the people of Hamburg, for all their long links with the new enemy. It did not spare Max Warburg. He had dreaded the thought of war with England and had done his best to stop it. But there was a price he would not pay—he would not countenance the humiliation of Germany or the concession of any of what he considered his country's vital interests. For it *was* his country. His bank, he knew, might—and indeed did—suffer great harm. But above all, he was a German patriot.

CHAPTER FIVE

Paul and the Federal Reserve Board *1895–1914*

THE meteoric rise of Max Warburg in Hamburg was paralleled, but in a different way, by the career of his brother Paul in New York.

Paul Warburg, born in 1868, the third son of Moritz and Charlotte, was Max's junior by only a year. They shared the same rabbinical education, and the same religious taboos instilled by their parents. But the two men were in temperament poles apart.

Paul started his adult life as apprentice to the London firm of Samuel Montagu, followed by a two-year period with the Banque Russe pour le Commerce Étranger in Paris. A further apprenticeship with his banker cousins, the Günzbergs, in Saint Petersburg was never taken up, though the necessary permission for an alien Jew to work in Russia was granted by the Russian minister of finance.

Then, oddly enough, in the early nineties, it was Paul, not Max, who was given the chance by his father of a journey around the world, on which he kept an extensive journal. During this same period he wrote what his contemporaries considered a group of poems well worth publication. He destroyed both the journal and the poems.

All through his life he tried to hide his talents, but for all his efforts they shone through. Many years later, when he was publicly acclaimed as the real architect of the Federal Reserve banking system in America, he showed his modesty and his wit alike by shrugging off the praise with the remark, "I really don't know who was the baby's father, but judging from the number of men who claim the honor, all I can say is that its mother must have been a most immoral woman."

It was by accident—in the shape of his younger brother, Felix—that Paul became an American citizen. He arrived in New York in the wake of his brother's whirlwind and spectacular courtship of Frieda Schiff. He modestly played the role of best man. He came, he saw, and was conquered by Nina Loeb, whom he married a year later.

Yet even an extremely happy married life could not wean him from his old allegiance to his German family and the city of Hamburg in which he had been raised. He became an employee of Kuhn, Loeb in New York but at almost the same time was made a partner—and became a very active partner—in M. M. Warburg & Co. His abilities earned him a partnership in Kuhn, Loeb in 1902, but he remained a partner in Hamburg, resigning only in 1907. It was not until 1910 that he became—the impression is reluctantly—an American citizen. Unlike the great majority of German-Jewish immigrants he was loath to turn his back on his native land.

It was five years after his promotion to a directorship of Kuhn, Loeb that Paul Warburg made his first real mark on the American financial setup. In 1907 he published a pamphlet entitled *Plan for a Modified Central Bank.* The ideas and proposals it contained had long been fermenting in his mind. Its impact was revolutionary.

The United States at that time was controlled financially by no less than twenty thousand national, state, stock savings and private banks, and loan and trust companies. Among them there was a minimum of consultation and cooperation. The system—or lack of system—expressed the nineteenth-century American concept of free enterprise and the average citizen's dislike of centralization of any form or kind. Its chief apostle in the early days of the new

Republic had been Thomas Jefferson. Centralization would mean, the man in the street was sure, either government controls (politicians interfering in banking) or control by Wall Street (bankers interfering in politics). Neither alternative was acceptable. Perhaps adequate to solve the financial problems of an earlier, predominantly rural America, the existing setup with its lack of flexibility was totally inadequate to cope with the new problems of a booming and frequently bursting industrial economy. Financial panics and failures became as much the rule as the exception. A striking example occurred in 1907 with the failure of the Knickerbocker Trust Company and a run on the Trust Company of America.

Paul brought to the study of America's problems the fresh eye of a European who believed in, and had seen operated, "a system which permitted expansion and contraction to go to their very limits," the idea in fact of mutual aid developed through acceptance credits, with a maximum of international cooperation. A year after he had become a partner in Kuhn, Loeb he showed Jacob Schiff a memorandum advocating the adaptation of the European model to America's needs.

Schiff passed him on to James Stillman, president of the National City Bank of New York, who asked him, "Don't you think the National City Bank has done pretty well?"

"Yes, Mr. Stillman, extraordinarily well."

"Why not leave things alone?"

"Your bank is so big and so powerful that when the next panic comes you will wish your responsibilities were less."

It came, and again, in 1907, Paul was summoned.

"Warburg, where is your paper?"

"Too late now, Mr. Stillman, what has been done can't be undone in a hurry. If reform is to be secured, it will take years of educational work to bring it about."

Paul was to be the chief educator, starting with his 1907 pamphlet, in which he advocated a central bank in Washington owned half by the government and half by the national banks.

There should be a salaried president and a board of directors "independent of politics—which by its composition would afford a reasonable guarantee that it would not be swayed by selfish motives." Central to the scheme was that the central bank should have the sole right to issue currency.

To start with, Paul found few supporters among either bankers or politicians. His pamphlets poured from the presses, and in one lecture at Columbia University he quoted a speech of Abraham Lincoln in his 1860 presidential campaign: "I believe in a United States Bank."

He soon became a national figure, and his correspondence with famous economists multiplied. In 1910 the Merchants Association of New York gave their support to his plan for a united reserve bank for the whole country, but the banks continued to resist. There was far less hardening of the arteries in commerce than in banking.

Nonetheless, his first real triumph came with his conversion of Nelson Aldrich. Aldrich was head of the National Monetary Commission in President Taft's Republican administration, to which Paul was also attached. He had been at first a rigorous upholder of the status quo. A visit to Europe dramatically changed his views. He summoned a group of experts, which included Paul, a senior partner in Morgan Grenfell, and the new president of the National City Bank of New York, to a private conference on an island off the coast of Georgia. If the rendezvous could not be kept secret, its purpose was. Ostensibly, this powerful group was on a duck-shooting expedition. Paul had never handled a shotgun in his life and had to borrow one.

A sidelight on Paul's rapidly growing reputation in these years —in 1902 he was only thirty-four and totally unknown in the country of his rather reluctant adoption—is a remark of the former President Theodore Roosevelt. In answer to one criticism of the proposed establishment of any form of central bank, that the United States couldn't find men able enough to manage such an undertaking, Roosevelt replied, "Why not give Mr. Warburg the job? He would be financial boss, and I would be political boss, and we could run the country together."

There is no more ardent a champion than a convert to a cause. Aldrich now went further than Paul and advocated a single central bank, which Paul deemed to be a political impossibility. Paul preferred to concentrate on limiting the number of Federal Reserve banks and establishing a single Federal Reserve Board.

His pioneering activities might have been interrupted by the return to power of the Democratic party under Woodrow Wilson in 1912. But informed opinion was now on Paul's side.

"Aldrich's conversion ended the period of education by individuals. Henceforth generalship was in the hands of the political leaders," Paul wrote in his memoirs.

An influential figure was Colonel E. M. House, whose influence over President Wilson foreshadowed that of Harry Hopkins on Franklin D. Roosevelt some twenty-five years later. It was House who ensured that Paul should play the leading part in drafting the bill to be sponsored by the two congressional committees headed by Senator Robert Owen and Representative Carter Glass.

This bill, known as the Federal Reserve Bill, became law in December, 1913. It provided for twelve regional Federal Reserve banks with a Federal Reserve Board sitting in Washington. It went more than halfway toward meeting Paul's desiderata—he was a master of the art of the possible. It became the cornerstone of a new financial system that ten years earlier would have been unthinkable, and which in its operation was to enable the United States to bear the enormous and manifold strains involved in its extraordinary economic expansion during this period.

In the summer of 1914 Paul Warburg was nominated by President Wilson as a member and vice-chairman of his own offspring, the Federal Reserve Board. At first Paul appeared surprisingly reluctant. He refused to appear before the Senate for confirmation of the appointment on the grounds that he was not a candidate for office. Then war broke out in Europe, and Paul withdrew his refusal and was immediately confirmed. He was to serve for four momentous years.

CHAPTER SIX

Felix: The Man in the Green Suit *1894–1914*

FELIX WARBURG, born in 1871 the fourth of Moritz Warburg's sons, reached New York on the eve of his marriage to Frieda Schiff in 1893. From the day of his arrival he set his heart and mind on becoming Americanized. He maintained the closest ties with his family bank in Hamburg, he paid many visits to Germany, but unlike his brother Paul, no thought of becoming a German-American commuter entered his mind. Like so many German Jews, he turned his back on his native land. Like Max he remained proud of being a Jew, but just as Max put Germany first, Felix aspired to be thought of first of all as an American citizen.

For a young man of his temperament, life with father-in-law in a strange land might loom as a difficult trial, and father-in-law Jacob Schiff fully intended it to be.

At first there was close supervision of the young couple. On their honeymoon Jacob assigned to them as chaperon one of his wife's personal maids. ("I spent my honeymoon with a German governess," Felix was later to comment.)

Jacob was appalled when, in the early stages of the honeymoon, Frieda became pregnant. He reacted strongly against the prospect of his child so speedily becoming a mother.

But the old ramrod had a softer side. "I cannot tell you how happy dear Mama and I are in your own young happiness," he wrote to them just before they returned.

Every Friday the Warburgs came to dinner at the Schiffs' house on Fifth Avenue for a Sabbath Eve celebration. These were solemn, stiff, and to the younger generation, very boring occasions. Jacob would read the traditional prayers, candles were lit, prayers were said, blessings given, family photographs kissed. But no younger Schiff or Loeb or Warburg, if he or she were in New York, would think of missing—perhaps "dare to miss" is the better phrase—these occasions. Jacob was still very much the domestic tyrant.

Prayers played almost as important a part in his life as the amassing of wealth. Felix was tolerant of this strict orthodoxy, but unimpressed. He and Frieda continued to observe grace at meals, light candles on Friday evening, and attend Temple every Sabbath they were in the city. If his attendance was, in his own words, merely *une acte de présence*, Felix never abandoned his religion. In the words of his son Gerald he became "a Jew who took the Jewishness out of American Jewry, an American patriot who believed in the Jewish faith."

Felix throughout most of his life was the most exuberant of all the Warburgs. In his very young days he—and Max too—had been regarded by Hamburg society as young blades. They drove, according to Frieda Schiff, a very dashing dogcart.

Felix was by instinct an expansive optimist. Between him and Max there was a marked affinity of character, if not a comparable flamboyance.

Much of the young blade of Frankfurt persisted after his re-settlement in the United States.

One day for example, he wore a stylish green suit to work. On the way downtown in the subway he met the head of the National City Bank.

"For heaven's sake, Felix! You look like Robin Hood."

Later in the day at a board meeting at Kuhn, Loeb a messenger burst into the room and handed Felix an urgent parcel. It contained a bow and arrow "with the compliments of the president of the National City Bank."

At the Metropolitan Opera he reserved two seats directly behind the conductor. So important a patron was he that when he was present the conductor for the night would turn and bow ceremoniously to him before picking up his baton. Frieda recorded in her privately printed memoirs that after the opera, "Our car was always first in line, for all the doormen and policemen were well acquainted with Felix and eager to receive his lavish tips." (Often, however, Felix had gone backstage to congratulate his favorite opera singer of the day.)

There is something rather appealing about Frieda's candor. So many people, now as then, revel in the *douceurs de vie* that only money can buy, and pretend they don't. The daughter of Jacob Schiff was well acquainted with the advantages of great riches; at least she was candid about it, and so indeed was Felix.

One day his wife bewailed to him that at their home in White Plains getting good fresh milk for the children was very difficult. "If only we had two cows."

In no time a complete herd of Guernsey cattle was chewing the cud in the White Plains pastures.

Among Felix's other indulgences was buying one of the first automobiles in the United States—a De Dion Bouton. His matched black horses won a championship at the Madison Square Garden Horse Show, and on his luxury yacht, the *Carol*, a typical meal would be lobster and squab, salad and cheeses, and white wine. In later years Albert Einstein was to be a frequent guest.

The White Plains estate had been acquired in 1904, and the decisive reason for its purchase demonstrates how easy it is for the very rich to indulge their whims.

The Felix Warburgs belonged to the White Plains Country Club. Complaints were made to Felix by some of its members about the excessive noise his offspring made. Very well, Felix would buy a plot of land adjoining and build himself a mansion.

THE WARBURGS

"Woodlands," as it came to be called, proved a most exceptional mansion. By architectural standards it is a monstrosity. Probably it can be most accurately described as a pile in the Scottish baronial style, a crenellated building topped by a great square tower.

The first item to be constructed was an indoor squash court, around which the rest of the house was formed. There was a huge greenhouse inside which was a swimming pool. There were stables for horses and carriages, and a grass tennis court where champions like Alice Marble, Betty Nuttall, and Helen Wills were invited to play. There was even a polo ground where, to judge from movies of the time, Felix and his children disported themselves with much enjoyment but a considerable lack of skill. Most startling of all was a garage, the first garage to be built as part of a house. Felix had great difficulty insuring a house which included a room for a combustible machine.

Felix's original purchase was rapidly expanded until his estate covered seven hundred acres of what was then pastoral, wooded countryside. On it houses were built for his mother-in-law (the widow of Jacob Schiff), for his oldest daughter, Carola, and for his Russian relations, the de Günzbergs. His brother Paul and his sister-in-law Nina built their own house nearby, calling it "Fonteney" after a street in Hamburg where they had lived when they were first married. Today, Woodlands is used by a kindergarten, and of the original houses, only Paul's now survives. A wooden frame building resembling a Swiss chalet, it is in sharp contrast to Woodlands, which is the home of a genial country landowner. It is sporting-pastoral and might have existed in one of the richer English shires. Felix's townhouse was equally stately.

In the first thirteen years of their marriage he and Frieda lived on East Seventy-second Street; then they moved to 1109 Fifth Avenue. This ornately facaded mansion, built, to Felix's requirements, in the François Premier style, today houses the Jewish Museum, but for the most part it remains as it was when Felix and Frieda with their daughter and four sons lived in it. Five stories high, it is built around a huge stairwell that rises uninterrupted the whole height of the house, guarded by a heavily carved oak balustrade. On the second floor were two rooms that housed some of Felix's most beloved possessions—his collection of early German woodcuts, including the work of Cranach, his Italian prints, and his etchings by Dürer and Rembrandt.[1]

He was an amateur of the arts, seeking good advice and taking it.

On the second floor of Number 1109 was the big dining room, hung with tapestries, and the conservatory, with mullioned windows, a famous Botticelli, and on a prie-dieu, a book that Felix believed to be beyond price— his beloved Wittenberg Bible.[2]

Also on the third floor was the music room. There was an Aeolian pipe organ, specially adapted to electric Pianola rolls, from which came the children's first experiences of grand opera. The room had a painted ceiling and massive crystal chandeliers. The walls were lined with rare books. There were wrought-iron lamps and Gothic sculptures. Here Felix would arrange concerts for his friends. They sat on small—and very uncomfortable—gilt chairs and listened to string quartets and soprano solos.

For the young friends of Felix's children, entry to Number 1109 was a formidable affair. Double glass doors framed in bronze with Gothic decorations led to the big entrance hall, which, to the eyes of an eleven- or twelve-year-old, seemed to be awash with liveried footmen. All seemed formal and outsized, and they were glad to scuttle up to the fourth floor where the young Warburgs spent the greater part of their holidays.

A feature of this floor was the electric railway set that serpentined from room to room. Below were their mother's and father's apartments, where from her boudoir Frieda wrote to each child every day they were away from home.

---

[1] Now in the Metropolitan Museum of Art.

[2] After his death it was discovered that it was not, as the experts had told him, Martin Luther's original copy. But so wonderfully executed was the forged signature that the Library of Congress, to whom in perfect faith his widow had offered it, asked to be allowed to keep it as an outstanding example of the forger's art.

Felix's letters were less frequent, dealing in practical matters, often admonitory, occasionally laudatory—the letters of a man anxious to be proud of his offspring, sometimes doubtful whether he would be.

Proud of them, on occasions such as the arrival of school reports, he might not always be, but devoted to them he certainly was. He was their constant playmate, revealing a streak of almost childish naiveté. It was Frieda who fussed.

"Why is it," he once asked her, "that my children are so wonderful, and yours seem to be so full of troubles?"

Later, when his sons had grown up, Felix used to emerge from 1109 Fifth Avenue flanked by all his sons. Five abreast they would march down the avenue for several blocks greatly impeding the flow of uptown pedestrian traffic. Felix was always inclined to the grand manner.

But in the offices of Kuhn, Loeb the grand manner deserted him. He had neither the patience nor the talent for the intricacies of merchant banking. Indeed, he treated the whole question of money so cavalierly that on one occasion he sent his fifteen-year-old son on a holiday in the confident expectation that the boy would be able to cash Felix's traveler's checks.

Felix disliked the whole atmosphere of bearded expertise he was surrounded by, and his father-in-law at work always scared him.

As a more-than-middle-aged man, he was showing a friend around the big partners' room at Kuhn, Loeb on Wall Street. In a small inner sanctum could be seen the shrunken figure of Jacob Schiff, then in his eighties. Suddenly from the sanctum came a short bark. Felix was being summoned. He almost scuttled to obey.

Felix was involved, however, in one of Kuhn, Loeb's most important decisions, even if it was a negative one.

Bereft for a few days of any partner to advise him, Felix was forced to interview the Swedish match king, Ivar Krüger on his own. Armed with an effusive letter of introduction from Max Warburg in Hamburg, Krüger was seeking Kuhn, Loeb's backing for his rapidly pyramiding schemes. Felix hedged, avoided any commitment, finally suggested another financial house.

Actually, he was only following orders. Max had sent him a letter as well, advising him to have nothing to do with this highly suspect entrepreneur. Not long afterward the Krüger empire crashed.

This one swallow could not, however, make a banking summer. Felix totally lacked the commercial shrewdness, expertise, and caution that had enabled his Warburg forefathers to build up slowly and unspectacularly a solidly prosperous business. Nor did he possess the eye on the main chance that had enabled Jacob Schiff to become the presiding miracle worker of Kuhn, Loeb and a multimillionaire.

Yet when still a young man he was very rich. No figures are available of his wealth at any time, but his style of living and the size of his benefactions speak for themselves.

His income at least must have been very large, made up from his share in the profits of Kuhn, Loeb, and from another more private source. One of his sons, asked how his father had become so wealthy, replied succinctly, "He married the boss's daughter."

He was rich, and he was bored by his work at the bank. The outcome might have been his emergence as a talented, popular dilettante, for while lacking any formal training he had a real love of the arts and he liked to live surrounded by creative people and beautiful objects.

The small change of conversation eluded him, and as a host he preferred to listen rather than expound, but on occasion he displayed a considerable wit:

"Children should be obscene but not absurd."

"I am like Heinz's pickles, I belong to fifty-seven varieties of committees."

He confided to Einstein one day, "Everything is relative except relatives, and they, alas, are constant."

He was also a man of great energy and force—when the fancy

took him. In the years before World War I he took on many duties.

He was treasurer of the American Museum of Natural History, and he is commemorated by the Felix Warburg Room, which contains a remarkable display of the ecology of southern New York State. For many years he was on the boards of the Metropolitan Opera House and the New York Symphony Orchestra. He helped James Loeb (Paul's brother-in-law) to found the Institute of Musical Art that became the Juilliard School of Music.

All these activities, however hard he worked at them, could still be described as those of a rich amateur. But his dilettantism had a more sober side. His work as a member of the New York City Board of Education included insisting successfully that nurses be assigned to duty in the city's public schools, developing a special program for retarded children, and starting the first probation system for young offenders ever to exist in New York City.

During this period Felix also began his very successful career as a fund-raiser. He always made sure that any individual or organization to whom he was appealing for funds was made aware of the amounts that friends and rivals had contributed. "If you want to get money out of people," he would say, "you must be very careful to remember their first names."

Critics might say that these manifold activities, however time-consuming, were only a sort of soul tax to ward off accusations of frivolity and ostentation, but Felix's subsequent career was to prove his sincerity. In his youth and early middle age he displayed a vast capacity for enjoyment. He was always a little larger than life. He was to remain so, but in his later years—in certain significant ways—he was succeeded by a different Felix.

CHAPTER SEVEN

Max: The Uncrowned King of Hamburg

1914–29

WORLD WAR I broke out on August 4, 1914. In the United States Paul Warburg had recently been appointed vice-chairman of the Federal Reserve Board, and Felix was mixing philanthropy and pleasure in White Plains and on Fifth Avenue. Eastward across the Atlantic, Sir Edward Grey, the British foreign secretary, announced "the lamps are going out all over Europe."

Amid the encircling gloom, Max Warburg was heavily engaged in those early weeks both in Berlin and Hamburg considering a series of makeshift schemes to take the place of the thorough economic preparations for war which he had vainly advocated since 1908.

It is often claimed that in both world wars the Germans entered the fray armed to the teeth both militarily and economically while the democracies faced them in total disarray. In 1939 this was a fact, but in 1914 it was a myth. The army was ready, and that was all—Max's had been a lone voice on the economic front. The Kaiser and his advisers staked all on a knockout blow based on the fatally modified Schlieffen Plan.[1] The German defeat at the first battle of the Marne a month later revealed the basic weaknesses at home.

By August 6 Max and Ballin were on their way to Berlin by car—all trains had been commandeered by the military. In Berlin emergency discussions took place:

Was it possible to commandeer American merchant shipping? There was none within reach.

Could the government raise a loan in America?

Max strongly urged a mission to the United States headed by the colonial minister. The fact that he had two powerful banker brothers in New York may have raised in him false hopes. Anyway, bureaucratic delays made it certain that when the minister finally crossed the Atlantic the chance, if there had ever been one, had vanished.

Should there be a moratorium on debts? It was decided that this was an impossibility—a view that Max had always strongly held. Instead, a series of "war-credit banks" was set up to help firms and industries that the outbreak of war had thrown into financial danger. Warburgs formulated the rules and regulations that should govern such banks. The first was organized in Hamburg, and all the other war-credit banks throughout Germany followed Max's rules.

His advice, in these early days of war, was much in demand—he was at the center of things. He did not long remain so. The war was to be run not by bankers and economists but by generals and admirals, by Ludendorff and Tirpitz, with the Kaiser as their figurehead. Max's influence rapidly became peripheral.

He was sent instead on foreign visits—to Belgium to negotiate, with considerable success, with the Americans about relief for the populations under German control, whose treatment by the German military was alienating neutral opinion; to Bulgaria and Rumania; to Sweden several times, where he had powerful banking

[1] The Schlieffen Plan was for a wide, encircling movement through the Low Countries. Under political pressure it was modified to exclude Holland. As a result, the Belgian Army remained intact and the Allies had a shorter line to defend.

connections as well as relations who might persuade the Swedish to an interpretation of neutrality more favorable to German interests. As Max ruefully commented, "To persuade Sweden to enter the war on our side I knew to be an impossibility."

Such missions convinced him how misguided his country's political conduct was and what fateful consequences it would bring in its trail. Quite early the patriot began to have misgivings.

He was consulted in 1915 by Tirpitz's deputy on the advisability of unrestricted U-boat warfare. He was vigorously opposed. It was certain to antagonize American opinion, and it was vital to keep America neutral. On the other hand, if America joined Germany's enemies, unrestricted U-boat warfare might be essential to avert defeat. Max's approach to this question was strictly pragmatic.

The year 1916 was one of stalemate. For the first time Max had doubts about victory. It may be that he was already entertaining thoughts of a negotiated peace. He can be excused for thinking that *total* victory by either side would delay, perhaps forever, a return to the world of international finance in which he had grown up and prospered. But his underlying optimism buoyed him up. As he recalled in his memoirs:

I worked meanwhile very hard at my business. Despite all the alarms and difficulties our undertakings were by no means on the rocks. We had for a long time had the idea of founding a business which would make Hamburg even more than before the center for the financing of foreign undertakings.

We hoped in this way—*if we ever got out of the war*—to utilize the expertise of overseas houses [author's italics].

In 1918, in fact, he founded the *Aktiengesellschaft für In-und-Auslandsinternehmungen* ("joint stock company for home and foreign undertakings"), linking several big German firms, with a capital of 25 million marks.

If we ever got out of the war.

In March, 1918, Max was sent by the government on a peace

mission to Holland. In the same month Ludendorff launched his great, and nearly successful, offensive in the West.

Once again, after three and a half years of stalemate, German armies stood almost at the gates of Paris.

The intention was for Max to meet with an American envoy who, it was hoped, would take the initiative. He did no such thing, and Max returned empty-handed from a totally abortive mission, only to be accused by Ludendorff and others of having attempted to treat with the enemy. The unjustified accusation, obviously prompted by the fact that he had two brothers who were American citizens, would never have been made against a non-Jew.

Earlier, before the United States entered the war, Max had been offered a far more important mission than those in Belgium, Sweden, and Holland—the post of ambassador in Washington. He refused it, "perhaps rather high-handedly."

The reason he has given to posterity was that, though he would always be a leader or colleague in concerns that interested him, he would never be an overseer in a deposit bank that had no connection with its head office.

But he might not have been telling the whole truth. In those days ambassadors had real powers and responsibilities.

A more likely reason for his refusal was the presence in New York of his brothers Paul and Felix. For the German Foreign Office this may have been why they had offered him the post. But for Max the personal conflict which would have arisen must have seemed intolerable.

The embarrassment for his brothers of his presence in Washington would have been intense. In this instance, perhaps, family feeling took precedence over German patriotism.

Yet another post was to be offered to him.

In the final weeks of Germany's collapse in the autumn of 1918 Prince Max of Baden was called in as chancellor. Max had known the prince well for many years and admired him greatly. In early

October 1918 Max had arranged a meeting in his suite at the Adlon Hotel in Berlin between the prince and Ludendorff.

The two men, he decided, lived in different worlds, but the world of Ludendorff was panic-stricken while the world of Prince Max remained sane. With Prince Max at the helm, President Wilson might be persuaded to order a cease-fire and to save Germany from the ultimate catastrophe.

It was a vain hope, and Prince Max lasted only a few weeks.

But during that brief tenure he offered Max the post of finance minister. Max refused, telling the prince that the German people would never suffer a Jew in that position. Assimilation had not gone that far. By his refusal he may have avoided the fate of a fellow Jew, Walther Rathenau, who became foreign minister and was shot down in the street three years later by right-wing assassins.

On November 11, 1918, an armistice was signed in a railway coach in the forest of Compiègne, by which the German representatives agreed to what amounted to unconditional surrender.

Ten days earlier Kaiser Wilhelm, the "supreme warlord," had fled into exile in Holland.

Between those two dates chaos spread to many parts of Germany. On November 5 a revolutionary workers' and soldiers' council seized power in Hamburg. The leaders summoned Max before them. Negotiations took place over a meal in the Rathaus. How, they demanded to know, did he think the treasury bonds the leading bankers and industrialists of Hamburg held could be renewed?

Max replied, "Just as before," which meant "through the usual channels," which in turn meant considerable delay.

Max knew that without this renewal the revolutionaries had at their disposal little more than 60,000 marks. He knew also that at a word from him the authorities in Berlin would ensure instant renewal.

"You don't seem to know where the power now lies," he was told.

He knew very well the threat behind such language, but against the advice of colleagues fearing for their lives, he held firm.

We sat, the two opposing parties, together, watched over by lethally armed sailors, at a long table, and all ate together with spoons from a huge soup tureen. Outside was a frightening, noisy crowd. After the meal we stood at the window, watching a downpour of rain, and I wondered whether and how we should survive.[2]

That the family and the firm did so was largely due to Max's firmness during days of negotiation, until the new regime collapsed. It was a fine example of the value of delay.

Five days after the armistice Max was asked by the new government in Berlin to lead the finance delegation to the peace talks at Versailles. Max agreed to serve on the delegation but nominated Carl Melchior as head in his place.

Originally a judge, Dr. Melchior had been appointed to M. M. Warburg & Co. as its permanent legal adviser. When Paul Warburg had finally left Hamburg in 1902, he had taken Paul's place as Max's chief confidant and in 1917 had been made a partner in the firm, the first man outside the Warburg family ever to achieve that status.

He came to be regarded by, for example, John Maynard Keynes, as the ablest as well as the most palpably straightforward of all the Germans at the conference.

Melchior became not only the finance delegation's leader but a full member of the German peace delegation as well.

Why Max Warburg performed this act of apparent self-abnegation has remained a mystery. Did he, the head of Warburgs, who had always led from strength, doubt his abilities as a negotiator from weakness? He may have feared the not unlikely appearance on the American delegation of his brother Paul. He may have been reluctant to expose himself and his firm to criticism if too harsh a settlement were imposed on the German people.

[2] Memoirs of Max Warburg, 1952, Hamburg, Germany.

According to his own account Max went to Versailles hoping that the German delegation could settle for "reparations only to the limits of possible payments and for the rest participation of foreign interests in German industry and enterprise." He admitted that further cession of German colonies might be necessary.

It would almost certainly have been better for the world if Max's hopes had been fulfilled, but can he really have believed, after the events of the previous four years, after the horrors of trench warfare, after Allied casualties mounting into millions, that anything comparable could be achieved? If so, he was living in cloud-cuckoo-land—but a sunny optimism was always a factor in his makeup.

Any illusions he may have had about Versailles must have been dispelled by the initial reception the French gave the German delegation. They were treated less like delegates than prisoners of war.

On their arrival by train at a wayside station the delegation was met by the head of the French detachment detailed to guard them. The station was ringed by French troops.

Max got into the waiting car and sat on the back seat. He was told rudely by his "overseer," a Lieutenant Henry, to sit on the jump seat.

The Hôtel des Reservoires, where they were to be billeted, seemed full of soldiers with fixed bayonets. It was also icy cold.

When Max and his companions wanted to take a little constitutional after lunch, it was at first forbidden. Later the prefect of police arrived. "Your wishes," he declared with mock geniality, "have been anticipated by the French authorities. Follow me." They were taken to the Bassin de Neptune in the park of the château of Versailles and shown a space sixteen meters long by four meters wide. This was to be their cage. His companions wanted to protest, but Max advised them, "Isn't it better to leave ill alone?"

Later matters improved, and they were given the freedom of half the park. Armed supervision ceased, but if they wanted to seek out the press in their neighboring hotel, they must proceed through a fenced-off alley.

Max took these restrictions more calmly than his colleagues. He quickly realized that in modern times chivalry toward the vanquished was not the order of the day. The whole incident was in its petty way an example of French yearning for revenge.

The events that led to the final signing of the Treaty of Versailles are common knowledge—the inter-Allied squabbles, the defeat of President Wilson's idealism, the obduracy of Clemenceau, the diplomatic skills of Lloyd George, the mounting despair of the Germans.

For Max the outstanding figure among the Allied delegates with whom he conferred was the British economist John Maynard Keynes:

> On the inter-Allied Finance Commission Keynes was by far the most gifted. At the close of a session he gave us the opportunity always to give him our joint impressions. He was an obvious seeker after the truth. Understanding and insight marked his every word. When he abruptly left Versailles Melchior and I said to each other that he had wearied of the insanity of the negotiations.[3]

Keynes later confirmed this view, as he was amply to confirm Max's verdict on him.

In the spring of 1919 Max shuttled frequently between Versailles and the finance ministry in Berlin. A key problem was the lifting of the Allied food blockade—partially solved by Melchior's offer to place 100 million marks out of Germany's slender gold reserves at the disposal of the Allies.

On food Max found himself negotiating with one of Clemenceau's most slavish minions, a Comte de Lasteyrie of the French finance ministry.

At the end of one session de Lasteyrie asked Max what Germany would do when she had finally to yield to French demands.

[3] Memoirs of Max Warburg.

Max replied, *"Nous allons faire faillite"* ("We shall have to default").

Taken aback, de Lasteyrie was silent, and Max began to leave.

"And France?" he asked as Max reached the door.

There was no answer.

"La France"—Max chose his exit line with care—*"La France fera faillite un jour plus tard que nous"* ("France will default one day later than we").

That very day de Lasteyrie demanded that Max be replaced—*"Celui-ci est trop impertinent"* ("That one is too impertinent")—to which the reply was that the German delegation possessed no one less impertinent than Max.

Some years later de Lasteyrie made known through an emissary that he would like to talk with Max. The suggestion was not taken up, and the temptation to say "I told you so" was resisted.

By then, after the collapse of the French currency, "it had become clear to de Lasteyrie that the Treaty of Versailles had been a disaster for France as well." [4]

It was a treaty that Max finally refused to sign. In June the German finance delegation advised its government to reject the final Allied terms, and Max was a party to this advice.

He persisted where the rest finally gave way. In his view, "To sign the Treaty would be to ensure the economic ruin of Germany."

It could well have been, and for a while in 1922 when the French attempted to enforce reparations to the full by occupying the Ruhr, the center of German heavy industry, it seemed that it had been.

Max could not foresee in the atmosphere prevailing at Versailles that in a matter of years the Americans and British would be only too anxious to come to the rescue of the country they had condemned to economic death.

After the experience of Versailles Max returned to his task as head of M. M. Warburg, with Melchior once more his number-two man.

[4] Memoirs of Max Warburg.

THE WARBURGS

In that same year negotiations took place among the largest German banks about setting up an international clearance bank. The advice of John Maynard Keynes was sought and given, and in 1920 Warburgs in collaboration with the House of Mendelssohn in Berlin founded the Deutsche Warentreuhand AG.

A hundred million marks' worth of shares were issued for the biggest electrical undertaking in Germany, twenty-five million shares being taken up by Guggenheims of New York.

It was the beginning of the flood of American money that was to pour into Germany in the years to follow.

Relations with his brothers had been reestablished in August, 1919, when Max and Paul met in Saint Moritz and discussed the problem of the repayment of Warburgs' foreign debts. But the lifeline that Paul was shortly to throw to his brother, and through Warburgs to German industry in general, belongs more to the story of Paul.

The reunion between the two brothers at Saint Moritz is mentioned dispassionately by Max in his memoirs as a meeting at which business was successfully discussed. Paul has left no written record of it at all.

Yet it must have been an emotional occasion. World War I had torn the first rent in their solidarity. After the United States entered the war in 1917 all communication between the German and American Warburgs ceased. Between Paul and Felix in America and Max (and Fritz) in Germany there had sprung up a barbed-wire fence that none of them wished to scale. Their Jewishness was temporarily overridden by their loyalty to the country of birth or of adoption.

It was in these early postwar years that Max saw more of Dr. Hjalmar Schacht.

This rising young man was called in by the comparatively democratic Weimar government to stabilize the mark after the French occupation of the Ruhr and the disastrous inflation that followed in 1923. He succeeded brilliantly, became known as a "wizard" of finance, and was appointed president of the Reichsbank.

His "wizardry" appealed to Max's liking for the bold gesture and for taking innovating risks. Schacht also had many contacts in Germany's ruling hierarchy. It was at a lunch in 1924 given by Schacht that Max met Germany's new, and very old, president.

Field Marshal Paul von Hindenburg's name was becoming revered in Germany, as the shock of defeat wore off, as a symbol of a glorious past. The feeling was already growing that the soldiers had been let down by the politicians.

Max's memory was not so short, and his first meeting with the president filled him with profound melancholy. He was to revise his opinion, recording later that he had judged Hindenburg quite falsely and that Gustav Stresemann had shown fine insight in backing him.

It was also during these years that Max first met Chaim Weizmann, destined to be the chief architect of the State of Israel. Max had been active in Jewish relief circles during the early stages of World War I: "At the request of New York friends (among them, Felix Warburg) I interested myself in the succor of the unhappy Jews in Poland and Galicia." [5]

Max sent Carl Melchior to investigate. The result was an interdenominational committee set up with Polish cooperation and backed by massive American funds.

At this time the German government was eagerly courting American goodwill—Gentile or Jewish—and raised no objections.

Max had been less successful in his efforts to help the Jews in Palestine. He had besought the foreign office in Berlin to let the Turks know, when they became Germany's allies at the end of 1914, that it was important that Palestine should be left "in some form or another" to the Jews. The foreign office did seek from the Turks a letter to that effect, but to no avail. There was to be no Turkish "Balfour Declaration."

[5] Memoirs of Max Warburg.

Now, years later, Weizmann sought to make Max take the Zionist viewpoint. In the ensuing arguments the latter's young daughter Gisela passionately took Weizmann's side. In 1928 Max was persuaded to pay his first visit to the Holy Land. He returned, perhaps half-convinced by Weizmann's arguments; at least he founded in Berlin the first German branch of the Jewish Agency. But for Max the affairs of Germany were always paramount, and at this time he could be excused if he was more concerned with anti-Semitism in Germany than with pro-Semitism in Jerusalem.

After the murder of the Jewish foreign minister, Walther Rathenau, Max received a warning from Hamburg's chief of police —threats had been made against his life. He would be wise to show himself in public as little as possible and not to go into restaurants.

Yet these anti-Semitic clouds seemed to have passed with the advent to power of a new foreign secretary, Gustav Stresemann, and above all with the signing of the Treaty of Locarno in 1925.

The Locarno Pact was signed by Britain, France, Germany, Italy, and Belgium. It provided for a mutual agreement not to wage war against each other and to underwrite the existing provisional status of the Rhineland as a demilitarized zone. It also involved the immediate admission of Germany to the League of Nations.

It seemed to almost everyone in Western Europe and the United States to return Germany fully to the community of nations and to guarantee at least a generation of peace.

In the light of Locarno it is not surprising that in his memoirs Max Warburg gives to the chapter dealing with 1926 the heading *Scheinblüte* ("deceptive bloom").

He also refers to it as the year of greater understanding.

Germany, now a member of the League of Nations, was prospering, with flourishing new enterprises, new amalgamations, in many of which Warburgs played their entrepreneurial part.

Carl Melchior was chosen as the only German member of the finance committee of the League of Nations. At the bank on Ferdinandstrasse the good times seemed to have come again, and the major planet in the bank's constellation was once again Kuhn, Loeb.

When the first transatlantic telephone was opened in 1928, Max was the second German to use it: "Apart from personal greetings to brothers Paul and Felix, we put through a Foreign Exchange transaction of three million dollars with the International Acceptance Bank." [6] It was more than a new toy, for it was very useful in speeding up financial deals.

At Kösterberg, Max and Alice were surrounded by a happy family, with the swimming pool and tennis court fully employed. Fritz and his wife Anna had their own house on the estate.

His oldest brother, Aby, released from his sanatorium,[7] was a frequent visitor, as were the American brothers, Paul and Felix. Max was unquestionably the uncrowned king of financial Hamburg.

Did Max convince himself that everything was as it had been in the balmy days before the war? Did this political conservative really reconcile himself to the social-democratic policies of the Weimar Republic? His radical leanings were shoots of a tender plant, nurtured perhaps by fear. But ostensibly the sun shone on Warburgs' enterprises even more warmly than it had done in the century's first decade.

In 1928 partners in M. M. Warburg & Co. held directorships in no less than eighty-six firms—Czech, Dutch, Austrian, American, as well as German. In foreign affairs Max was an ardent supporter of Gustav Stresemann, whom he regarded as primarily responsible for the Treaty of Locarno. Max described Stresemann's death in 1929 as "a severe loss to Germany and to all who seek a new and better world." It was a sentiment shared by bankers the world over, to whom peace was an essential premise for profit.

But on the home front? No member of the Jewish faith could view with equanimity in the late 1920s the increasingly ominous

[6] Memoirs of Max Warburg, 1952, Hamburg, Germany.
[7] See Chap. 12.

alternative to the Weimar Republic, except perhaps for Max Warburg. He seems to have had few apprehensions. In fact, as a banker he had become bitterly critical of the existing regime.

At the time he confided to his diary words that could be uttered today by many industrialists the world over:

> So long as we are under the scourge of such high taxation a strong, workmanlike development of Germany is impossible. We [Warburgs] have had in the last years an extraordinarily high turnover, but if we omit windfalls, which have nothing to do with the health of a firm, then we must state that our firm, with today's taxation, is not in a position to advance our business further.[8]

Did he realize that, taxation or no taxation, there was "something rotten in the State of Germany"? That the seeming prosperity was based far too much on loans and credits—above all, on American money? If so, he faced the gathering storm with that remarkable optimism that was one of the keys to his character.

In 1929 he created a new firm in Amsterdam. It was a break with tradition, the first time a Warburg firm had been created outside the confines of Hamburg.

In the same year his son Eric became a partner in M. M. Warburg & Co., the fifth generation in direct descent to hold such a position. Ring in the new, but by no means ring out the old. There was plenty of fight in Max Warburg yet.

[8] Memoirs of Max Warburg.

CHAPTER EIGHT

Paul: The Cassandra of Wall Street *1914–32*

PAUL WARBURG was, as we have seen, appointed vice-chairman of his own brainchild, the Federal Reserve Board of the United States, in the summer of 1914. Six weeks later war broke out in Europe. Sooner than he thought, the enormous financial strains that he had anticipated the country of his adoption would have to bear as she advanced to commercial predominance in the Western world were imposed, while the country of his birth embarked on a war with Britain, France, and Russia supported only by the suspect strength of Austria-Hungary.

What was Paul's attitude toward the belligerents at this stage? Like the great majority of Americans he did not advocate, he did not even anticipate, American participation in the struggle. But if he had thought it inevitable or even likely he might well have pressed for an alliance with Germany. His roots were in Germany; he spent as much of the year as he could in Hamburg, first at his house at Gross Fontenay, then, after he had sold it, at Kösterberg.

His wife insisted, as long as it was possible, on importing German servants from Kösterberg and on keeping in close touch with the German ambassador in Washington.

The Loebs came from Cincinnati, the most German of all American cities. Paul's favorite brother Max was head of a German banking firm and an unequivocally patriotic citizen. How could he be expected to be fervent about anything but neutrality?

He was ardent in his support of his President's policy of standing on the sidelines and striving for a peace without victory for either side. His attitude could be summarized in the words of another German-born American, Elmer Davis, who in the opening months of the war wrote in the magazine *Forum:*

> I am neutral with the bitter soul-searing neutrality of the man whose reason tells him one thing while his emotions cry out the other. . . . I think I can see a heavy majority of arguments in favor of the Allies; and yet I feel no joy over their successes. When von Kluck swept on from Ons to Lille, and then on to St. Quentin, Compiègne and Senlis, my blood boiled up and sang. Tannenberg and Coronel were to me personal triumphs, though I knew all the time that my enthusiasm must be repented in the chill, gray logical dawn of the morning after.[1]

It was this agonized neutrality that caused Paul's temporary estrangement from his only and much-loved son, whom the world came to know as Jimmy.

In 1914 an undergraduate at Harvard, Jimmy had spent all his formative adolescent years in America. He had been happy on his childhood visits to Germany, he was fond of his uncle Max and his German cousins, but he was almost, if not quite, second-generation American, and Harvard, where he was studying, with its long-forged intellectual links with Britain, was violently pro-Ally.

"Although my German blood," Jimmy was to write later, "at first 'boiled up and sang' over the initial German victories, I did not for long share my father's admiration for Wilson's policy. . . . In my newly acquired feeling of Americanism I could no longer root for the German Army." [2]

---

[1] Elmer Davis, "Concerning Fatherlands," *Forum* (March, 1915), Vol. 53, pp. 304–314.
[2] James P. Warburg, *The Long Road Home* (New York, 1964), p. 31.

Instead, he listened to, and applauded, the trumpetings of his boyhood hero Theodore Roosevelt, when he condemned "the skulking cowardice" of neutrality and "the evil wickedness of the Kaiser."

Therein lay the difference.

Jimmy was becoming Americanized, as to a great degree was his extroverted uncle Felix. His father, the sensitive introvert, could not yet, if ever, make the choice. For all his great services to the country of his adoption, he remained at heart, of all the American Warburgs, the most German. And when in the spring of 1917 America did enter the war, Paul was faced by the agonizing fact that in his own words "brother must fight brother."

A few months before America's entry into the war, Jimmy volunteered as a flying cadet in a newly established naval air station. By then Paul's neutrality had ceased to be so ingrained. The unrestricted U-boat warfare, so strongly if pragmatically condemned by his German brother Max, had tilted the scale toward the Allies. Nonetheless, he was still at heart opposed to war and furious that his son should anticipate what only his mind told him was inevitable.

A man of great moral courage, he condemned also what he considered in Jimmy to be a display of physical exhibitionism. To fight on demand was one thing, to anticipate the demand was folly.

Not long afterward, it was Jimmy's turn to be angry. War had been declared, and Jimmy had high hopes of being sent overseas to see active service. To his fury he discovered that his father had intervened with the Secretary of the Navy: Jimmy was grounded at home.

Paul's vice-chairmanship of the Federal Reserve Board was due to expire in August, 1918, but it was in President Wilson's power to renominate him. In the summer of that year no one could foresee the imminent collapse of Germany. In June, Paul wrote to the President:

THE WARBURGS

Dear Mr. President,

On August ninth my four-year term of office as a member of the Federal Reserve Board will expire. I do not know whether or not, under the constant burden of grave and pressing decisions, you have reached the point where you wish to deal with the question of naming my successor, or whether or not you contemplate to have me continue in this work. Nor would I presume to broach this question were it not that I felt that, in consequence of recent occurrences, it has become one of policy rather than of personalities.

Certain persons have started an agitation to the effect that a natural-ized citizen of German birth, having near relatives prominent in German public life, should not be permitted to hold a position of great trust in the service of the United States. (I have two brothers in Germany who are bankers. They naturally now serve their country to the utmost of their ability as I serve mine.)

I believe that the number of men who urge this point of view is small at this time. They probably have not a proper appreciation of the sanctity of the oath of allegiance or of the oath of office. As for myself, I did not take them lightly. I waited ten years before determining upon my action, and I did not swear that "I absolutely and entirely renounce and abjure all allegiance and fidelity to any foreign potentate, and particularly to Wil-helm II, Emperor of Germany," etc., until I was quite certain that I was willing and anxious to cast my lot unqualifiedly and without reserve with the country of my adoption and to defend its aims and its ideals.

These are sad times. For all of us they bring sad duties, doubly hard, indeed, for men of my extraction. But, though, as in the Civil War, brother must fight brother, each must follow the straight path of duty, and in this spirit I have endeavored to serve during the four years that it has been my privilege to be a member of the Federal Reserve Board.

I have no doubt that all fair-minded and reasonable men would consider it nothing short of a national disgrace if this country, of all countries, should condone or endorse the attitude of those who would permit the American of German birth to give his all, but would not trust him as unreservedly and as wholeheartedly as he, for his part, serves the country of his adoption. Unfortunately, however, in times of war, we may not always count upon fair reasoning. It is only too natural that, as our casualty lists grow, bitterness and undiscriminating suspicion will assert themselves in the hearts of increasing numbers—even though these lists will continue to show their full proportion of German names.

Much to my regret, Mr. President, it has become increasingly evident that should you choose to renominate me this might precipitate a harmful fight which, in the interest of the country, I wish to do anything in my power to avoid and which, even though resulting in my confirmation, would be likely to leave an element of irritation in the minds of many whose anxieties and sufferings may justify their intense feelings. On the other hand, if for reasons of your own, you should decide not to renominate me it is likely to be construed by many as an acceptance by you of a point of view which I am certain you would not wish to sanction. In these circumstances, I deem it my duty to state to you myself that it is my firm belief that the interest of the country will best be served if my name be not considered by you in this connection.

In writing you this letter, I have been prompted solely by my sincere conviction that the national welfare must be our only concern. Whatever you may decide to be best for the country will determine my future course. We are at war, and I remain at your orders.

May your patience and courage be rewarded and may it be given to you to lead our country to victory and peace!

Respectfully and faithfully yours,

PAUL M. WARBURG

The letter crystallizes what agonizing problems World War I posed for the Warburg family.

Brother must fight brother, each must follow the straight path of duty.

Max and Fritz were German patriots; Paul and Felix, once the United States entered the war, had no choice but to regard their brothers as enemies. Communication between the two families ceased.

Paul's resignation was accepted by the President, and he returned to Wall Street and Kuhn, Loeb.

Of the part he had played in creating the American Federal Reserve system *The New York Times* wrote: "His own modesty and self-effacement insured that he never asserted the claim, familiar in most of such public undertakings when they have achieved success, of having been the originator of the plan. In actual fact he had a more legitimate title to that distinction than any other American citizen." No longer a government employee, Paul devoted his energies, once the war ended in November, 1918, mainly to the formation of what even more than the Federal Reserve Board was his own particular brainchild, the International Acceptance Bank. The impulse behind this scheme was the paramount need to pump new blood into the hardened arteries of international trade. It was in the spring of 1919 that Paul launched his idea.

While the Allies were browbeating defeated Germany and quarreling among themselves at Versailles, he was planning what his son has called "a sort of bankers' bank, to be owned by leading American and European banks and also private bankers, which would specialize in financing international trade by means of bankers' acceptances issued under letters of credit."

A feature of the bank would be to introduce the principle of two-name bank acceptances so that the liquid reserves of the banking system should be strengthened—always one of his main preoccupations.

But he had another preoccupation.

It would be an exaggeration to say that the International Acceptance Bank was conceived primarily as a rescue operation, but the plight of his brother Max in the midst of the shattered German economy was very much on his mind. His scheme was, in brief, a gesture of "hands across the sea," with a special hand extended to the Hamburg firm of M. M. Warburg & Co.

The International Acceptance Bank, finally incorporated in 1921, had as shareholders the Svenska Handelsbanken and the Skandinaviska Kreditaktiebolaget, representing Sweden; Sir Ernest Cassel, the National Provincial Bank, and N. M. Rothschild & Co. for Britain; the Schweizerische Kreditanstalt of Zurich and Dreyfus Söhne & Cie. of Basel for Switzerland; Hope & Co. and the Nederlandische Handel Maatschappig in Holland; and M. M. Warburg & Co. With all the participants, Warburgs already had, from prewar days, the closest connections.

The International Acceptance Bank was an attempt, for a time successful, to substitute international monetary cooperation for commercial anarchy. It was certainly the chief means by which M. M. Warburg & Co. recovered a great measure of its prewar fame and prosperity.

That this prosperity was to prove illusory, and not only for the Warburgs, was due in part to the American impulse, allied to a genuine altruism, to "get rich quick," and the failings of politicians faced with an upsurge of nationalism.

Paul Warburg was among the first, if not the first, to predict the world depression and the implications for the future of the International Acceptance Bank. In the late 1920s he was reviled as a Cassandra for prophesying a break in Wall Street's bull market. He told all who would listen that the castles they had been building out of paper profits on the stock exchange were constructed not of brick but of rapidly shifting sand and that boom would turn into slump. He advised all his friends to sell their shares while there was still time.

He died, in 1932, while the prophecy was still being fulfilled.

It has been said that he died of a broken heart.

The Wall Street crash did destroy all that he had striven for. He was also deeply disturbed by the predicament in which the financial crash of the previous years had placed his brother's Hamburg firm.

Certainly he was resentful that his advice to Max to liquidate had been rejected. He had in fact been overruled by his son Jimmy and had subsequently sacrificed a sizable part of his personal fortune in a rescue operation.

But a man who had achieved so much, who had shown such moral courage, who was so deeply committed to life in all its aspects, could not die, however disappointed, of a broken heart.

He had lived quietly and unostentatiously. His modest house

next to his brother Felix's estate at White Plains is a striking contrast to Felix's flamboyant Gothic horror. He was a connoisseur of music and literature; his refinancing of the famous Loeb Classical Library founded by his brother-in-law, James Loeb, entitles him to a niche in the literary pantheon. His impression on his contemporaries was profound.

On his death Walter Lippmann wrote: "He was wise, far-seeing and upright. He was one of the chief architects of what is strongest in our central banking system and the truest critic of its weakness. He foresaw the latter, he spoke out in time, no one could ask a better epitaph."

As for his place in the family history, he—and Felix too—epitomized a special Warburg loyalty.

Writing in 1933, Max described them as "my brothers, who always regarded my fate as their own."

❦ CHAPTER NINE

Felix and Palestine: The Brighter Dream?
1914–38

WHEN World War I broke out in August, 1914, Max Warburg was the leading banker in Germany, with close international banking and commercial links to leading financial concerns in Western Europe, Japan, and the United States. Paul Warburg was vice-chairman of the Federal Reserve Board in America. Felix Warburg, in contrast, lagged far behind, and in stature he never, perhaps, matched up to either of them.

By this time Felix had established a reputation as a fund-raiser for charitable purposes, able to charm money out of almost anyone.

Numerous American-Jewish charities had benefited from his activities, but for the most part these charities had been acting entirely independently. Within the city limits of New York, seventy-five separate organizations were engaged in Jewish relief.

It was Felix's achievement to organize them into a single body, with the title of Federation of Jewish Charities, of which he became chairman. More than forty individuals were found to underwrite the very large reserve fund that he deemed necessary for the federation's activities. The Federation's success led to its imitation in virtually every Jewish community across the country.

But compared to his brothers' achievements this was very small beer, well within the compass of any rich man of ability who was philanthropically inclined.

It was in 1916 as the first chairman of the Joint Distribution Committee (JDC) that Felix stepped onto the stage of world Jewry.

The inspiration for the JDC was the plight of the East European Jews. For centuries the Jewish inhabitants of this vast area had lived under the threat of a pogrom. When war came in 1914 the threat once again became actual, its horrors exacerbated by wartime conditions. Famine stalked the Jewish settlements.[1]

The cries for help were heard the length and breadth of the United States but initially by mutually hostile bodies. They were the rich Jews of New York, proud alike of their German cultural heritage and their American citizenship, and the far poorer orthodox Jews whose attitudes and practices were still those of the East European communities (the *shtetlach*) from which persecution had driven them. Then there were the Jewish Socialists, who, like their European brethren, believed all too fondly that out of war must come the triumph of socialism everywhere. And finally there was that small but already influential group, the Zionists.

It was Felix's achievement to weld these potentially hostile groups into allies pursuing a common cause.

In *The Saving Remnant*, Herbert Agar wrote: "If one man can be given the chief credit for building a strong and lasting machine out of such unlikely material, it is Felix M. Warburg of New York." [2]

The main inspiration—and the chief source of funds—of the JDC was German-Jewish. It is to Felix's credit that its initial activities were marked by his determination that they should be di-

---

[1] The harsh uncertainties, the threat to property and even to life among which they lived, have been recently illustrated on the musical comedy stage. *Fiddler on the Roof* ran for many years both on Broadway and in the West End.

[2] Herbert Agar, *The Saving Remnant* (New York, 1960), p. 19.

rected as much to the succor of Polish and Russian as of German victims.

In a recent book about the Jewish "aristocracy" of America, *Our Crowd*,[3] Stephen Birmingham implies that this German-Jewish clan that had been established for half a century or more in their adopted land kept aloof from later East European ghetto immigrants, fearing that they would undermine their own hard-won acceptance in American society.

If there was any truth in the insinuation, Felix Warburg worked wonders in the JDC to refute it. Shortly after the organization's founding, an article appeared in the newspaper *Jewish World*, stating: "When the general indifference of the majority of Jews in America in this great calamity is considered, then the money, nearly six hundred million dollars, which these three committees [the components of the JDC] have collected proves that their work was wonderful, colossal—and successful." Felix remained its chairman until 1932, by which time it had branched all over the world.

He was also instrumental in founding the United Jewish Appeal that was responsible for the co-ordination of international fund-raising for its two major partners, the J.D.C. and the United Palestine Appeal, founded in 1925. The title of the latter is significant; it marked a shift of emphasis away from the ideal—the helping of all Jews everywhere—which had inspired Felix when the JDC was conceived. The shift was accelerated by an event that took place on November 2, 1917. On that day the British government issued, in what looks retrospectively like a fit of absence of mind, its famous Balfour Declaration.

The full text read as follows:

His Majesty's Government view with favour the establishment in Palestine of a National Home for the Jewish people, and will use their best endeavours to facilitate the achievement of this object, it being clearly understood that nothing shall be done which may prejudice the civil and

---

3 Stephen Birmingham, *Our Crowd* (New York, 1967).

religious rights of the existing non-Jewish communities in Palestine or the rights and political status enjoyed by Jews in any other country.

The various interpretations—and it was capable of many—put upon the Balfour Declaration have bedeviled the relations of Jew and Arab in the Middle East ever since. On a lower scale they were to bedevil the friendships of Felix Warburg with many American and European Jews. These men and women, inspired above all by the siren calls of Chaim Weizmann, translated the phrase "National Home" as "National State." Since the British government at that stage of World War I was busily wooing Arabs as well as Jews, it is unlikely that it meant anything of the kind. But Felix, as chairman of the JDC, had to face increasing demands that the funds this organization was raising should be earmarked for the colonization of the Holy Land.

In the years that followed the Balfour Declaration the leaders of world Jewry were divided, like Caesar's Gaul, in three parts:

There were the maximalists—the whole-hog Zionists demanding an independent State of Israel. Their champions were Chaim Weizmann, and much later, David Ben-Gurion.

There were the minimalists, the cultural Zionists, those who envisaged Palestine as the home not of the Jews but of Judaism. Representative of these was Judah Magnes, first president of the Hebrew University of Jerusalem.

And there were the non-Zionists, the men who considered Jews as citizens of the world rather than of any particular Jewish State. Their standard-bearer was Felix Warburg, and of necessity his main foe was Chaim Weizmann.

Weizmann was Felix's foe because in the end their views became irreconcilable—but also a close friend. In conversation they struck sparks from each other, but on many matters they collaborated. Long after they had taken up their opposed positions Felix could still make a speech in Weizmann's honor at a public fundraising dinner.

Weizmann was a man of great brilliance and magnetic charm. He fascinated Felix and mesmerized Felix's wife Frieda. He was a frequent visitor to their mansion on Fifth Avenue and to their country estate at White Plains. Return visits were paid to Weizmann's London home on Addison Road.

Felix's public life was dominated after the end of World War I not just by the affairs of the JDC but by two new concerns, the Hebrew University of Jerusalem and the Jewish Agency for Palestine.

The foundation stone of the university was laid on the crown of Mount Scopus by Weizmann in July, 1918. In 1924 Felix paid his first visit to Palestine (according to Weizmann, at *his* instigation) and gave half a million dollars to the School of Jewish Studies, out of which the university grew. The original board of governors included, besides Felix and Weizmann, Sir Alfred Mond (later Lord Melchett), James de Rothschild, Albert Einstein, and Rabbi Judah Magnes. It was Felix's influence that secured for Magnes the post of university president.

From its earliest days there was controversy over the proper functions both of Magnes and of the university. Magnes was chief rabbi of the liberal Temple Emanu-El in New York, which had the wholehearted support, financial and otherwise, of Felix and his family. Up to the U.S. entrance into the war in 1917 Rabbi Magnes had been famous both as preacher and administrator. But during the conflict he used his oratorical gifts to preach all-out pacifism and fell into disfavor. He was forced to leave Temple Emanu-El and went with his family to Israel.

Felix had stood by him and, greatly influenced by his idealism, kept in touch with him during Magnes' voluntary exile.

Therefore, when the controversies over the university's true function began to grow and fester, Felix and Magnes supported each other.

The root of these controversies was in part semantic: a sincere difference of opinion about the meaning of the word *president*. To

Felix and Magnes it meant the man who ran the show—the general American interpretation—which would in effect allow Felix, through Magnes, to be the boss.

To Weizmann and the British Jews concerned, the title was honorary. No one would expect the chancellor of Oxford or the rector of Edinburgh to be more than a well-known figurehead.

But the disagreement went deeper than that. In Felix's opinion the university should be a cultural center for all the Middle Eastern peoples. As Magnes wrote in 1928: "Everywhere else in the world Jewish studies are in a corner apart. At the Hebrew University they are at the center of humanistic learning."

The view of Weizmann and his Zionist supporters was rather different. For them, the purpose of the university was not only to concentrate the study of Judaism, but to act as a political weapon for Zionism.

Felix had already sensed this as early as 1924. In a letter to Norman Bentwich, then attorney general for Palestine under the British Mandate, he attacked Weizmann for trying to pack the general committee that was supervising the university's birth pangs with "Zionists of the old tradition."

He went on fighting for his interpretation of the university's function right up to his death, and in general his wider view of what the university should stand for prevailed. Weizmann was forced to set up his own separate foundation for learning, the Weizmann Institute. Every effort to get rid of Magnes failed, including those conceived jointly by Weizmann and Einstein.

In his lifetime, and after his death, Felix was regarded by many as the supreme conciliator, the chairman who could reconcile every point of view and by doing so get the best possible results. (He used to say: "The talent is to get the honey out of even the sour flowers.") Such were the opinions of men like Herbert Agar, Norman Bentwich, and Nevile Laski.

It was not only money that he could charm out of people, it was forgiveness. Meyer Weisgal, Weizmann's chief aide and fund-raiser, once discovered that Felix had written a letter about him of an extremely contemptuous and disparaging nature. Nonetheless, he always referred to Felix as really a very charming man.

But in matters which concerned him very deeply, or about people to whom he felt committed, Felix could be a tough and bitter fighter. Judah Magnes, as president of the Hebrew University, had his faults—Felix would never hear a word against him, he was Felix's man, and that was that. His correspondence, where anything Palestinian was concerned, is full of acerbity.

I am frank to say [he wrote at the end of 1925 to Judge Julian Mack, a fellow but more moderate non-Zionist] that whatever joy I might have felt in helping the university to get under way has been very much dampened at the last meeting. . . . I am afraid that having received the financial support in the U.S.A. they [Weizmann and his supporters] are now trying to make out of this university an international debating society.

For this outburst he was rebuked by Judge Mack, who condemned his "intemperate refusal" to realize that they were only at the beginning of a great new enterprise and so there was bound to be undue sensitivity on all sides.

In the same year Felix wrote to Magnes:

The J.D.C. has shaken off the Zionists, but only by my talking to Dr. Wise (which I had not done for three years) like a dutch uncle. It was disgusting to see how Wise turned round and for the sake of being considered a good boy, revised his attitude entirely. I doubt if the J.D.C. will give much more money to Palestine as the behavior of the Zionists at the meeting disgusted people who were there.

There is not much conciliation here; rather there is more than a touch of condescension.

This condescending attitude, if usually overlaid with charm, is displayed in a further incident. Again it concerned Meyer Weisgal. In the midthirties Weisgal was masterminding the production of an epic musical history of the Jewish people, to be directed by Max

Reinhardt. Money was urgently needed to finance the venture. A meeting was arranged between Weisgal and Felix.

Felix told him he didn't believe in this venture (which in the end left all concerned a great deal poorer), but added graciously, "I don't want to hurt you. I know that every Jew in New York is going to ask you if Warburg is with you, and I don't want to give these people an excuse not to help you."

He gave $10,000 and authorized Weisgal to make the gift public.

Felix's second and more important preoccupation was the Jewish Agency for Palestine. This had been provided for by the British when they agreed to act as the mandatory power for the region in 1922. It was assumed by Jews all over the world, though not made explicit by the British, that it would be a sort of shadow government.

Seven years elapsed, however, before it came into being, a delay caused mainly by arguments between Zionists and non-Zionists. At last, in 1929, a representative council for the Jewish Agency in Palestine was formed, together with an executive committee, and set up in Jerusalem, with branches in London and New York.

Felix was a member of the council and chairman of the Agency's administrative committee and, usually by proxy, chief spokesman for the non-Zionist faction in Jewish affairs. A powerful member of the executive committee, holding views very close to those of Felix, was Maurice Hexter.

In 1927 a Joint Palestine Survey Commission had been set up under the auspices of the mandatory power. At that time Hexter was a professor at Harvard. Felix persuaded the dean of the university to release him and secured his appointment as secretary to the commission.

He did more—he made it financially possible for Hexter to accept the job. In a typically generous gesture made easier by his wealth he handed him two sealed envelopes on the day he was to sail for Palestine. One contained a letter of credit to cover his expenses in Palestine (his salary would be minimal). The other, another letter of credit for "anything you don't feel like charging to expenses."

It is therefore understandable that two years later, when Hexter became a member of the Jewish Agency's executive committee, Felix assumed his protégé would, if called upon, execute his desires. Once again there was a problem in semantics. To Felix, Hexter was an "executive" who would "execute" the wishes of the parent board. But to the members of the executive committee "executives" were men who gave the orders that in the last resort Felix and his fellow members of the representative council must carry out. It was fortunate for their continuing friendship that Felix and Hexter so seldom differed on policy.

In the early days of the Jewish Agency, efforts were made by both Felix and Weizmann to find common ground on Palestinian matters. For all their differences of opinion these two men had the interests of the Jewish community totally at heart.

In a letter of November, 1929, Felix nags at Weizmann, telling him he "still wants to save pronounced principles rather than make a terribly uncertain situation certain and liveable." But in an admission that at the time everyone was pulling in opposite directions, he adds, "There must be complete harmony and one chief. I am willing to resign as Chairman of the Administrative Committee. You are President of the Agency. I feel that you must, so far as possible, be made into a Mussolini." (In the light of subsequent events in Italy it was an ironic role to assign to him.) He went on, "If I am without authority in this country [America] and if the Zionist Organization of America is an independent body free to do what it pleases, then I feel that the efforts that you and I and others are making can lead nowhere."

Weizmann replied tartly that the Zionists in America were subject neither to the Jewish Agency nor to Felix nor himself.

On one issue, however, the two men could agree. After the Arab riots of 1929 the British government imposed fresh restrictions on

Jewish immigration into Palestine. Both Felix and Weizmann resigned their posts in protest. The British promptly had second thoughts, changing their tactics—of settled policy toward Palestine, Ramsay MacDonald's minority labor government had none. Felix and Weizmann consequently resumed their posts.

A year later Sir John Hope-Simpson, who had headed a commission of inquiry into the riots sent out from England, wrote to the colonial secretary in London:

There are extensive changes in prospect in the circles of the Jewish Agency. The American group, represented outstandingly by Felix Warburg, do not at all approve of the way in which matters have hitherto been run. It is desirable that both the Commanding Officer and the High Commissioner should maintain the closest touch with this Group.

There was no doubt that the British were backing the horse that would give them the least trouble. Felix could be very difficult if he was thwarted, but in 1930 he was of the British persuasion—Palestine should be a home for the Jews, but not the site of a Jewish nation.

As he told Lord Melchett in 1929: "I am for action which shows we want to reach agreement with the Arabs, and for action which expresses our reduced ambitions plainly."

Specifically, he told Melchett that the Agency should press for the commutation of the death sentences passed on Arab participants in the recent riots. Melchett's reaction was violently hostile. The battle lines between Zionist and non-Zionist were becoming clearer.

Felix was indeed a conciliator between Jew and Arab, but he was also a prime mover in raising money for the Emergency Relief Committee, headed by Hexter, that assisted Jewish victims of the recent riots. In connection with this committee, Felix nearly made a financial blunder. He was responsible for depositing the $3 million raised in the United States in the Fifth Avenue Bank of Manhattan. During the mounting atmosphere of financial panic of 1931, there were rumors that the bank was approaching insolvency.

He had the bright idea of transferring the money to the Deutsche Bank in Germany, whose head was his old friend from the Joint Palestine Survey Commission, Oscar Wessermann. The transfer was effected, making funds in marks available as required in Palestine. Then the German government, now under Nazi control, forbade the export of currency. Advised by Max Warburg, Hexter approached the high official in the government in Berlin who dealt with foreign exchange. He received no comfort, so he decided to test his man.

He left on the official's desk, as if by accident, an envelope addressed to himself containing the equivalent of about $1,200.

"If he was honest," Hexter explained many years later, "no harm would be done. If not, I could do a deal."

The official wasn't honest, and Hexter arranged for a credit of $5,000 to be ready for him on call in London. Subsequently, the Deutsche Bank was instructed to make funds available for Palestine, and the situation was saved.[4]

Felix waged many battles over Palestine in the years that followed, right up to his death. He was often skeptical about his opponents' aims. In 1932 in response to a remark by Hexter about the impracticality of the Zionists, he said, "I am certain that if the [Jewish] Agency had money for one new colony [5] the movement would decide to create two and trust to the future to complete them."

On another occasion Felix privately stated his belief that if the State of Israel ever came into being it would be coming cap in hand every year to Kuhn, Loeb for another loan.

His autocratic attitudes were displayed in his refusal in 1932 to

[4] Within a year the high official left the country. Perhaps he foresaw the future under Nazism more clearly than did Max Warburg.

[5] These "colonies" developed into the modern kibbutzim.

contemplate a more democratic method of electing non-Zionist members of the Jewish Agency, or was this a sign that he was coming to realize that he was fighting a losing battle?

Yet always he demonstrated an acute sense of what was possible and a desire for conciliation.

In a letter to Hexter late in 1933 he wrote: "After all, if I should be the High Commissioner and would see how near to boiling point the Arab pot is at this time I would naturally go slowly, and I only regret that our friends—and among them Weizmann—are speaking in such large terms about the possibilities of Palestinian immigration."

His more generous side reappears in his warm agreement with Hexter's rigorous opposition to the staging of protest strikes in Palestine, which, he declared, would only "squander a portion of the rapidly declining goodwill which we [the Jews] possess in the world."

Conciliation again is his objective when he protests to Weizmann in 1935, "So long as Jews crow 'Jewish State' and 'National Land' your efforts [to get on a better footing] will not be taken very seriously by the Arabs."

Conciliation, the search for accommodation with the Arabs, was the mainspring of Felix's thoughts and actions about Palestine in those days. Why should there not be a multiracial state with room for both nationalities? After all, they came from the same Semitic stock.

But did he think that he could ever bring Weizmann and the other dedicated Zionists around to his way of thinking? His correspondence is full of attempts to do so, some oblique, some direct. "We two could make the world safe for Jewry," is the implicit theme of these letters.

They were both, in their very different ways, figures of international importance, and if today the name of Weizmann is the better known, it is largely because he came out on the winning side. The State of Israel is his monument, while Felix's hopes of Jews and

Arabs living together in perpetual amity lie buried in the dust.

All of his children applaud and support the new state which their father thought doomed to failure. Yet to a non-Jew surveying the Middle East today, the thought may occur that Felix had had in those early days of the struggle for Israel the brighter dream.

But why was such a dream possible for Felix and impossible for Weizmann?

One explanation: their totally different backgrounds. Weizmann was born in the small town of Motol, in a remote corner of the Jewish Pale of Settlement created a hundred years earlier by Catherine the Great and comprising a wide area of Western Russia and Eastern Poland. It was a region utterly isolated from the outside world, redolent of the pogrom and where even in "normal" times Jews lived in a permanent state of semipersecution. Motol had streets of a kind, but they were unpaved, and all the buildings were of wood. Weizmann's father, though not poor by the standards of the time and place, had to support his family on an income of perhaps $150 a year. His occupation as a transporter of timber was extremely hazardous. For his son the only possible security for the Jews was their own state ruled by themselves.

Felix in contrast was brought up in one of the richest cities in Europe. The streets of Hamburg were paved, its houses solid brick and mortar. Felix's father was a prosperous banker. In these circumstances it was possible for Felix to imagine a bright future for the Jews as citizens of the world. It would be nice if they had a home in Palestine, but surely not essential.

To Weizmann such an attitude was anathema. In his autobiography *Trial and Error* he makes a bitter attack on the leading Jews of pre-1914 Germany. "They were the usual type of *Kaiser-Juden*, like Albert Ballin and Max Warburg, more German than the Germans, obsequious, superpatriotic, eagerly anticipating the wishes and plans of the masters of Germany." [6]

6 Chaim Weizmann, *Trial and Error* (New York: Harper Brothers, 1949), p. 143.

To such a man all Gentiles—Arab, British, American, French, or German—were always the potential enemy.

The final break between the two men was, in retrospect, inevitable—between Felix the American Jew with the emphasis on *American* and Weizmann the Jew with no other emphasis whatever. That it was so long delayed was due to the mutual fascination they exercised over each other.

Weizmann wrote in his autobiography:

[Felix Warburg] He was a man of sterling character, charitable to a degree, a pivotal figure in the American Jewish community, if not in very close touch with the rank and file. There was something of *le bon prince* about him.... I found [at a luncheon at Kuhn, Loeb's offices] an extremely affable and charming gentleman, very much the *grand seigneur*, but all kindness.[7]

And in an account of a later meeting, when Weizmann fondly thought he had converted Felix to Zionism, he wrote: "...it laid the foundations of a lifelong friendship which stood the strain of a good many differences of opinion."[8]

Perhaps Weizmann never knew that as far as Felix was concerned that friendship was irretrievably broken a few months before his death. It is the opinion of Felix's sons and of his closest friend and collaborator, Maurice Hexter, that after the events of the conference of the Jewish Agency at Zurich in the autumn of 1937, he would never have spoken to Weizmann again.

This conference was called to consider the report of yet another Commission on Palestinian Affairs, headed this time by Britain's Lord Peel. It was also the year of Edward VIII's abdication to marry Baltimore's Mrs. Wallis Simpson.

"I am sure," Felix wrote to Weizmann, "the Royal Commission will be delighted to get your evidence in a straightforward way in the King's English. But I am not so sure that the King's English is

[7] *Trial and Error*, p. 309.
[8] *Trial and Error*, p. 311.

quite the best that can be produced just now. They say it is under the strong influence of a Baltimore accent."

This was a lighthearted overture to what proved to be, for Felix, a tragedy. The commission recommended the abolition of the British Mandate and the partition of Palestine into separate Jewish and Arab states. This recommendation split the Agency.

Weizmann supported it, on the principle that half a loaf is better than none. At least statehood of a sort was being offered him. Felix, in poor health, attacked it.

In a violent, bitter speech he accused Weizmann of having lied to him. On previous occasions when they had discussed the matter he had always denied wanting statehood, Felix claimed. This volte-face was a disgraceful betrayal.

Since Weizmann in his autobiography makes no mention of this scene—or indeed of the Zurich conference—it is impossible to judge how justified Felix's accusation was. In any event he spoke for only a small minority. Acceptance of the principle of partition was overwhelmingly voted. Felix returned in despairing fury to New York and called an emergency conference of leading American Jews at a specially rented mansion on the banks of the Hudson River. Once again his passionate plea to renounce Weizmann and all his works was overwhelmingly defeated.

The *bon prince*, the flamboyant man in the green suit, was shattered. Three months later he was dead.

This end of the struggle between Felix and Weizmann was as inevitable as their rupture. The latter had the drive and force of a self-made man that Felix lacked. His career had been political from the start and motivated by patriotic Zionism. As director of the British Admiralty Laboratories in World War I, he had gained influence in high places and had the ear of many members of the British government, including the foreign secretary, A. J. Balfour, whom he had strongly influenced in the formulation of the Balfour Declaration. Against such a man, who was later to be acclaimed unanimously as the first president of the State of Israel, Felix's occasional victories could only be pyrrhic.

THE WARBURGS

If Felix's attitudes to the political problems of Jewry can be, and will continue to be, the subject of controversy, and if in such matters his financial generosity went hand in hand with a measure of intolerance toward those who opposed him, his sincerity cannot be called in question.

In other areas his reputation as a philanthropist is unqualified. He was tireless in helping others. In a single month in 1929, for example, he gave to twenty charities sums totaling over $60,000, involving the dispatch of over four hundred cables, telegrams, and letters. In addition, in that same month he gave $25,000 toward the encouragement of Jewish farm settlements in Russia, making his total contribution to that charity $125,000.

These charities, in many of which he was functionary as well as benefactor, included such odd bedfellows as the American Museum of Natural History, the National Committee on Prisons and Prison Labor, his sixteen servants at 1109 Fifth Avenue, the New York Kindergarten Association, the Nitchie School of Lip-reading, and $1,000 "To assist in the production of a Mr. Harper's play."

His public donations were matched by his private gifts and kindness. In the words of Maurice Hexter, "he was insanely generous." Not only generous, but thoughtful—in the grand manner.

He died, this man of many parts and many passions, of many faults and many virtues, in the Fifth Avenue mansion he had built and adorned.

❧ CHAPTER TEN

Max: Patriot or Victim?
1929–46

BETWEEN 1929 and 1931 the international financial structure built up after the signing of the Treaty of Versailles in 1919
collapsed in ruins. The collapse began with the Wall Street panic of
1929 when millions of dollars were wiped off the value of stocks and
shares. The tornado gathered force in Western Europe until, two
years later, the Kreditanstalt Verein of Vienna closed its doors. The
storm came near to destroying M. M. Warburg & Co.

American citizens had for years been "buying on margin," which
simply means buying shares with money they did not possess in the
expectation that the shares would rapidly appreciate in value.
When in 1929 a recession in business took place, there were count-
less bankruptcies and a total drying up of the sources for foreign
loans, and it was on those American loans that the postwar prosperity of Germany had been based.[1] In effect, German industrial
expansion proved to have been built on totally faulty foundations.

1 "The corner stone of German prosperity had been loans from abroad, principally
from America, and world trade. When the flow of loans dried up and repayment of
the old ones became due, the German financial structure was unable to stand the
strain." William L. Shirer, *The Rise and Fall of the Third Reich* (New York: Simon
& Schuster, 1960), p. 136.

Warburgs was at this time overextended. In order to achieve the rate of expansion of the previous few years, Max and his colleagues had borrowed largely from abroad, and particularly from the International Acceptance Bank. At times they had accepted large amounts of deposits. In 1930 the firm was due to repay 80 percent of its foreign loans and 50 percent of its domestic deposits. Could it take the strain?

The danger was plain to Max and to his partners, Carl Melchior and Dr. Ernest Spiegelberg. In 1930 he visited New York to discuss the situation with banker friends, in particular with his brothers Paul and Felix.

"When I went to New York in the Spring of 1930 I could foretell the coming economic crisis and was clear that my firm must concern itself with it. What I, like everyone else, did not foresee was the size and dynamism of the crisis." [2] Max's memory, when he wrote this, played him false. One man in New York had foreseen—his brother Paul.

Despite the threatening situation Max remained buoyant in his brother's presence. He "did lively business" with the International Acceptance Bank, was confident that if he could rely on the help of American capitalists whenever Warburgs needed it his firm could prosper even more than before. Paul and Felix were less sanguine. They had been taking a hard look at the situation and did not like what they saw.

"My brothers," Max wrote later, "were apprehensive not only of the economic but the political future of Germany, and feared for me personally and for Fritz and our families at the hands of the Nazis. They were opposed either to the firm remaining independent or even keeping its own name." [3]

It is unlikely that Paul and Felix were as prescient as all that. Three years were to pass before Hitler became chancellor. The

[2] Memoirs of Max Warburg, 1952, Hamburg, Germany.
[3] Memoirs.

threat to Warburgs was as yet only economic, not racial as well. Anyway, nothing fundamental was settled that year.

It was different in 1931, the year of calamity for businesses, big and small, all over the Western world. It was the year too when in Germany politicians of the stamp of Fritz von Papen and Kurt von Schleicher began juggling with the nation's fate to the advantage of no one but Hitler and his henchmen. It was then, surely, that Paul and Felix became concerned not only with the future of the family firm, but with their brothers' personal safety. They sent Paul's son Jimmy to Europe to investigate. What he saw he did not like— Warburgs was very heavily in debt.

There is perhaps a certain euphemistic tone about Max's recollections of this visit:

> My nephew James was in Europe in the summer of 1931, and brought my brothers' views into the open. He gave the most sympathetic attention to our views and as a result my brothers united with me in the ordering of our Dutch and American undertakings. . . . In the event, with the help of the family, our problems were solved. We went on from strength to strength.[4]

Did they? Max himself admitted later, in his financial report for 1933, that in the previous three years his firm's clients had fallen from 5,241 to 1,875. Edward Rosenbaum, in his highly sympathetic account of the firm under Max, stated: "Glancing through the papers covering the years from 1932 onwards we feel that the main springs of action are broken and that a tragic fatality overshadows 'the native hue of resolution.' "[5]

And what did "the help of the family" consist of? Jimmy reported back to New York that Warburgs was overextended to the point of approaching bankruptcy. Paul and Felix were at first inclined to let things slide. They felt they could do no more. Felix

---

[4] Memoirs.
[5] Edward Rosenbaum, "M. M. Warburg & Co. . . . ," in Year Book VII (New York: Leo Baeck Institute of Jews from Germany, 1963).

wrote to Max that it might be for the best if the firm went into liquidation. Max indignantly rejected the suggestion. When Jimmy heard of Felix's suggestion, he took his German uncle's side.

How could his father and his uncle contemplate the possibility of their family's firm, founded in 1798, with all its triumphs and traditions, ceasing to exist?

Paul and Felix thought again, and the firm was saved. It was saved, however, not by the International Acceptance Bank, nor by Kuhn, Loeb, but by the immediate pledging of Paul's and Felix's personal fortunes, much of which had rapidly to be called upon.

Thus, through the solidarity of the Warburg family, the continuation of M. M. Warburg & Co. was guaranteed and its independence preserved. Max was still at the helm. He still had the help of his brother Fritz and for a time of his young cousin Siegmund. Increasingly his son Eric played a part. Above all, he was flanked by Carl Melchior and Dr. Ernest Spiegelberg.

But when Melchior died in 1933, it was a major blow. For many years, Max was to maintain, he and Melchior had been regarded as "experts in many spheres." In particular, Dr. Hjalmar Schacht, president of the Reichsbank, valued their advice. Now Melchior had gone.

Still, in normal times the firm twice rescued by its American cousins might have flourished once more. After all, it had speedily recovered from the catastrophe of World War I. However, the times in Germany were very far from normal, and for Max and the whole Jewish population they became rapidly totally out of joint. Max could not have been entirely ignorant of this fact nor a little later, of the danger in which he personally stood. But his actions and his thoughts during the appalling years that followed the election in 1933 of Hitler as chancellor seem in retrospect to have been based on a false premise: "It can't be happening to me."

How *could* it be happening to the German patriot of World War I, the friend of the Kaiser, the man who had refused to sign the financial clauses of the infamous Treaty of Versailles, the uncrowned financial king of Hamburg, close to Schacht, the president of the Reichsbank, soon to become economics minister in Hitler's government, the man in fact who was a German before he was a Jew? There is something naive, almost pathetic, about this attitude, but also something heroic. Max decided, against the advice of many well-wishers, to ride the hideous Nazi storm until it blew itself out, in order to preserve, at whatever personal risk, the continuity of his beloved bank.

"I was determined to defend the firm like a fortress." [6]

In the last resort he believed he would have a lifeline in Hjalmar Schacht. The two men had worked together since the days of Versailles. As the financial wizard of the Weimar Republic in his position as president of the Reichsbank, Schacht had frequently consulted Max. Now he was scheduled to perform similar magic tricks on behalf of his new Nazi masters. Surely, as long as Schacht was near the seat of power, Max, even though he was a Jew, would be protected.

But Max seems to have overlooked the precariousness of Schacht's position. He was useful to his Nazi masters, but he held his post on sufferance and was not a member of the Nazi party. He felt himself too vulnerable to risk throwing the mantle of his protection over a Jewish financier. As economics minister Schacht lent the Nazis a veneer of respectability in the eyes of foreign powers. Max, with his outstanding reputation as head of M. M. Warburg & Co., provided a similar cover in international banking circles. For a while—a little while—Hitler needed to preserve the second of these assets, but the time would come when respectability was no longer needed and Schacht would be powerless—even if he were willing to save his Jewish colleague.

In 1933 the notorious Reichstag fire, stage-managed by the Nazis, was blamed on the Communists and the Jews and gave Hitler the chance to exclude the latter from all public offices, the

[6] Memoirs of Max Warburg.

civil service, journalism, teaching, and the stock exchange. The Nuremberg Laws of 1935 completed the legal exclusion of German Jews from public life.

The so-called Nuremberg Laws of 1935 deprived the Jews of German citizenship, confining them to the status of "subjects." It also forbade marriage between Jews and Aryans as well as extramarital relations between them, and it prohibited Jews from employing female Aryan servants under thirty-five years of age. In the next few years some thirteen decrees supplementing the Nuremberg Laws would outlaw the Jew completely. But already by the summer of 1936 . . . the Jews had been excluded . . . from public and private employment to such an extent that at least one half of them were without means of livelihood.[7]

Such was the world in which Max found himself living. When he protested about the Nuremberg Laws, Schacht assured Max that the laws related only to a minority of Jews, the peasants and the shopkeepers. He ended the conversation by asking Max to stop the hostile articles about the government that were appearing in British newspapers, particularly the *Manchester Guardian*.

On another occasion, a decision to demand Max's resignation from the board of the German-Atlantic Cable Company was reversed temporarily at the last moment by the Postmaster General. Schacht claimed that this request was due to his influence. In fact it was due to the violent protests made by an American member of the board, Averell Harriman.

Meanwhile, however, the pinpricks and insults had been gathering momentum. Max's friend Baron Schroeder gave him a message from the burgomaster of Hamburg. He hoped Herr Warburg would not take it amiss if in future he consulted him less frequently. One critical prop had been taken away from Max. He could no longer consider himself Hamburg's financial king.

Next, Schacht thanked him for past services and told him he was to be dismissed from the post he held in the Reichsbank. Then, in

[7] William L. Shirer, *The Third Reich*, p. 233.

1934 he was forced to resign his directorship of the Hamburg-Amerika Line.

This was a particularly bitter blow. Where now were the great days when he and Albert Ballin had made this company one of the wonders of the shipping world? He bore this setback with fortitude and wit. At a farewell dinner in Hamburg for himself and a fellow Jew who had also been forced to resign, he made an ironical third-person speech praising his own activities.

Still, Max remained in Germany, despite the increasing Nazi persecution.

He discovered that the authorities were having photographs taken of his activities to establish who were still his friends. Once revealed, these friends were warned not to see him again. He describes the process of isolation in his memoirs.

> Thus, I was boycotted. Only a very few Christians dared to speak with me. I was reduced to talking with the employees of the firm who still came to the Bourse. Many acquaintances made distant bows to avoid greeting me. We soon "liquidated" our Christian friends. Our first reactions were disdain and defiance. Next came the coming together of the family and Jewish friends. Never in my life had I read so much or concentrated so much on my paintings. Our employees and servants behaved splendidly. We had often to prevent them from expressing their rage at what was happening.[8]

The estate at Kösterberg was becoming a fortress against fear. Daily, Max was pilloried in the press. The vilest of the Nazi propaganda organs, *Der Stürmer*, run by the notorious Julius Streicher, accused him of collaborating with his American brothers to betray Germany at Versailles.

A caricature of him appeared, with the caption "Negotiator in Versailles, backer of social democracy. Jews, look at yourselves."

Max wrote in vigorous refutation to both the foreign minister,

[8] Memoirs of Max Warburg.

Baron von Neurath, and to his old friend Schacht. Neither was a Nazi, but neither replied.

Though Kösterberg had become a fortress it was still one from which it was possible to escape. Early in 1935 Max visited the United States in order to "regulate business arrangements with American friends." It was another way of saying that he was soliciting aid for German Jews. "I made a speech at a general meeting of the Aid Organization but could, owing to the fact that the Gestapo was watching, not say much of what lay in my heart." [9] Yet to the land of the Gestapo he willingly, courageously, returned.

Up till that moment Max had been living a bad dream he still hoped to be able to awaken from. Surely his beloved Germany would not long tolerate the horrors that had been imposed on it. Surely, so far as he personally and his bank were concerned, Hjalmar Schacht would see that he came to no harm. In his memoirs he records several conversations with his old friend in the next two years about the Jewish question but adds sadly that nothing came of them. Slowly his optimism faded, and he found himself on the road to despair.

"It was impossible," he wrote of the years 1936–38, "to carry on normal business, [it was like] a half death. In the first years of National Socialism it seemed to me that our business friends, many of whom were also personal friends, would have the means to offset such influences. I was wrong."

Yet he would not give in. Against all odds he fought for his Jewish compatriots. The days of Hitler's "Final Solution" (the total extermination of the Jewish race) had not yet come. It was still possible for Jews to buy themselves out of danger. For example, Warburgs set up the Palästina Treuhandstelle, which helped them get a better rate of exchange for the moneys, which, if they were lucky, Jews were allowed to transfer abroad. Such transfers were allowed in exchange for the increased purchase of German indus-

[9] Memoirs of Max Warburg.

trial products by Palestinian Jews. The Warburg bank in Amsterdam, not yet under the Nazi yoke, also rendered substantial assistance.

But two interrelated events in the spring of 1938 turned what had been only a bad dream into ineluctable fact. First, Max was summoned to Berlin by Schacht and told that his firm could no longer remain a member of the Reichsanleiche Konzortium, the cooperative organization of German banks on which the solvency of each member ultimately depended. When Max told the economics minister that in that case Warburgs would have to be liquidated, Schacht replied that he had anticipated that answer, but he had no further authority in the matter.

Max's comment in his memoirs is surprisingly free of rancour. "We said goodbye, after, for thirty years, we had in all possible ways worked together." [10]

Liquidation was, at least for the moment, avoided, but in the second major blow to the Warburg family fortunes, it was decreed by the Nazis that no Jews must in future hold any position in the firm. The firm was to be "Aryanized": Max must go, his brother Fritz must go, his son Eric and Dr. Spiegelberg must go.

But at this point some of Max's Christian friends reacted. A group of Hamburg bankers, industrialists, and merchants stepped in as caretakers. Warburgs' general manager, Dr. Rudolf Brinckmann, took Max's place as head of the firm. The Nazis cannot have been monitoring this maneuver, for if Dr. Brinckmann was not a Jew, he was a faithful and valued employee of M. M. Warburg & Co. He was also a director of Warburgs in Amsterdam. Dr. Paul Wirtz, a longtime friend of the Warburg family, would be at his side.

Was it a last attempt at international respectability in the eyes of the financial world that prompted the Nazis to insist that the firm should still be called M. M. Warburg & Co.?

[10] Memoirs of Max Warburg.

The experiment lasted less than three years. In 1941 the name was changed to Brinckmann, Wirtz & Co.

"In the circumstances," Max wrote in his memoirs, "I was happy that the name Warburg was removed from the firm."

In May, 1938, forty-six years after he had become a partner, Max made his farewell speech to his staff: "We had two choices. Either we could give the business up, go into liquidation and pass on what was left to another bank, or we could value the work we have done higher than the personalities concerned, sustain the firm, bow out ourselves and entrust the future to those who follow us." [11]

A few weeks later, with his wife and only son, he sailed for the United States.

It seemed to be the end. Fritz was already in voluntary exile in Sweden. His cousin Siegmund had left four years earlier. Of his four daughters Gisela accompanied him to America and was soon to marry an American lawyer, later to become famous as Judge Wyzanski. Lola, who had married the elder brother of the schoolmaster Kurt Hahn, would in a matter of weeks accompany her husband to England, and Renate was married and living in India. Anita had already moved to London.

The houses and the grounds of Kösterberg were empty, later to find employment as the site of an antiaircraft battery. Not a Warburg stirred in the offices on Ferdinandstrasse.

Max, however, could still not quite accept that it was the end. He told his friends in New York that he was only on a visit, that he had every intention of returning to Hamburg. The explanation he gave at the time for this decision was that his responsibilities for Jewish relief organizations were too great to abandon them altogether.

Throughout this period, critics had been saying that as long as Max Warburg had had access to Schacht he could indulge in the luxury of viewing the new German world as not totally evil. In

[11] Memoirs of Max Warburg.

planning to return to Germany *without* the assurance of Schacht's protection, Max was trying to prove his case, once and for all, even at the risk of his life.

He was saved from that risk by an assassination. On November 7, 1938, a young German-Jewish refugee, Herschel Grynszpan, shot and killed the third secretary of the German embassy in Paris. The Nazi reaction was immediate—a pogrom (which would be called *Die Kristallnacht*) such as Western Europe had not known for centuries.

Synagogues were burned, Jewish shops were looted, the concentration camps were filled almost overnight to overflowing, and no single Jew in all Germany could think himself safe from instant death. Faced with this outrage to civilization, Max knew that his return to Germany would be a folly that would be unmatched by any concrete results. Though he could not know of the instructions given by Reinhard Heydrich to the S.S. that "as many Jews, especially rich ones, are to be arrested as can be accommodated in the existing prisons" and subsequently dispatched to concentration camps, he needed little persuasion to conclude that such would be his fate. He stayed in America. He was never again to see his native land.

It has been said of Max Warburg by a harsh critic that this admittedly brilliant man "knew everything but understood little."

In the light of the achievements and successes of his earlier career, this verdict cannot be sustained, but so far as his last years in Germany are concerned it contains a grain of truth. He knew—he must have known—what the advent of the Nazis portended for himself and his co-religionists, but to the end he could not *understand* its utter and final significance. Intellectually, perhaps, he did; emotionally, never.

So he remained in Germany through most of the decade from the best of motives, despite all that was happening to himself and others. Only an assassination in Paris prevented him from returning to imprisonment and possible death.

He could not *understand* that there could be no question of recovery. Was it because he regarded himself as a standard-bearer for German Jewry?

Quite soon after Hitler came to power, Max's young cousin Siegmund, already a partner in the bank, understood what was bound to happen and decided to take himself, with his wife and child, to England. Max was furious and accused him of setting a bad example to his fellow Jews by running away. Siegmund had an answer ready. It was Max, not he, who was setting the bad example. It was Max who, by remaining in Hamburg, was raising false hopes in German Jewry by pretending that nothing was really happening. There is truth in the accusation. It is impossible not to admire Max's courage during those Nazi years. It *is* possible to doubt his wisdom.

Max lived to see the downfall of that Germany which he had come so reluctantly to hate. He survived to see a new Warburg firm spring up in New York under the initiative of his son and to take a major part in its success during the years when Eric went to the wars as a Combat Intelligence Officer in the U.S. Air Force. By 1941 both Paul and Felix were dead, and Woodlands and 1109 Fifth Avenue, which in the past had been to him almost second homes, were no longer in the family. But there were his two daughters in America, and his nephews and nieces, and the Warburgs were always a closely knit clan. His life had been exciting, often full of *Sturm und Drang.* Its closing years were calm. He died in 1946.

⚜ CHAPTER ELEVEN

Fritz: The Social Worker
1879–1962

OF THE sons of Moritz and Charlotte, Fritz Warburg was the baby of the family. Born in 1879, he was eight years younger than his elder brother Felix. Youngest sons normally do best in life when they break away from family tradition, and perhaps Fritz would have achieved greater fame had he done so. But it was not to be. Family tradition dies hard, and in due course he became first a trainee and later, in the early 1900s, a partner in M. M. Warburg & Co.

There are frequent references in Max's writings to Fritz's value to the firm. He was, his brother wrote, "a person who saw the kernel, the essential, in every man he met."

He was the conciliator, the man with the personal touch, invaluable in dealing with the increasing number of personal clients that the firm was increasingly acquiring, a man of compromise, capable of great patience.

In the words of Edward Rosenbaum, "His legal training,[1] his patience and his particular blend of both creative and critical sympathy made him the ideal, although sometimes too lenient, head of the firm's Credit Department."

[1] Legal training had often been considered advisable for scions of banking families. The present heir to Warburgs' studied law at Heidelberg University.

His older brother—who was also his boss—had a profound affection for him. Perhaps it was the attraction of opposites, for Fritz was never at heart a banker. As far as banking was concerned he lived in the shadows.

Fritz Warburg was a man of quite astonishing ugliness—he was compared with Toulouse-Lautrec—and of equally astonishing charm. One of his friends, later to become burgomaster of Hamburg, has recalled that if Fritz telephoned him any evening he would go at once to meet him, first turning to his wife and saying, "I'm sorry, but you won't see me again before midnight."

Culture, not business, was his forte, and it has been said that he would have been best suited to a contemplative life. Actually he probably would have been bored to death by such an existence. Culture to him was not only study—although he became a noted graphologist—but pleasure. He delighted in the theater and ballet —and in dancing, on which he prided himself.

Through the Warburg family as a whole, as in many Jewish families, there runs a strong strain of philanthropy. Fritz was no exception to this general rule, but his particular brand led him into places foreign to his brothers.

Between the bank on Ferdinandstrasse in Hamburg and the Warburg house at Kösterberg, there was, adjacent to the docks, the district of Saint Pauli. Through it Max Warburg and his family frequently drove, but it is doubtful that they ever stopped, for Saint Pauli is Hamburg's red-light district. If Max was the uncrowned financial king of Hamburg, Fritz filled the same position on the Rieperbahn, the main street of Saint Pauli.

In the early years of the twentieth century, the Rieperbahn was (and still is) lined with cafés and nightclubs of varying degrees of disrepute, frequented by sailors and ladies of the town. For the best possible motives, it became Fritz's habit to "cover the waterfront." For many years he ran a hostel there for the poor and destitute and became a well-known and well-loved figure in the district.

It was not, however, to the hostel but to another establishment he knew would serve good hot food that late one evening he took some boys from the famous Salem School.

These boys had just arrived from England where they had been sent to play a hockey match by their headmaster, Kurt Hahn (related to Fritz by marriage). Arrangements for their return misfired, and they finally reached Hamburg on a very dingy cargo boat, at a late hour. An SOS had been sent to Fritz to meet them. The crossing had been rough, and it was a bedraggled, woebegone group of teenagers whom Fritz took under his wing.

Seated at a long trestle table, the boys got their hot food, but the curtains that should have obscured the activities in the booths surrounding the room were in some instances inadequately drawn. For a man of the world Fritz was in this particular instance a shade unworldly.

In World War I, Fritz served for four years as commercial counselor for Sweden and Norway in the German embassy in Stockholm. While in this position he received peace overtures from a certain Protopopov, the financial expert of a Russian delegation returning from a visit to England.

With the approval of his Berlin masters Fritz entered into tentative discussions. Would the Germans consider, Protopopov asked, a separate peace, based on German recognition of that part of the old kingdom of Poland in German hands as an independent state? When it transpired that this suggestion was made without the knowledge even of the Russian minister to Sweden the conversations abruptly ceased, according to his brother Max, much to Fritz's chagrin. It was his sole excursion into diplomacy and no more successful than his brother's efforts in Holland two years later.

Fritz married a distant cousin, Anna Beata Warburg, in 1908. Of the two she was undoubtedly the stronger character.

For all his love of pleasure, throughout his life Fritz preferred the companionship of inward-looking men, of scholars and philosophers. Anna was an outward-looking woman, a pioneer in child education.

Enrolling as a young girl in the Froebel Training College in Hamburg, she later started the first *Volkskindergarten* in Germany, a preparatory school for young teachers. Later, her work in coordinating youth organizations throughout Germany brought her international fame. These activities came to an end when the Nazis came to power. They had their own ideas about youth, which were quite different from Beata's.

She and Fritz retired to Kösterberg, where they gave shelter to more than a thousand Jewish families awaiting the slender chances of being allowed to emigrate. At Kösterberg she started the first Jewish kindergarten, which, after the war, she reorganized in Israel.

Through the years from 1932 to 1938 Fritz stayed at his brother's side at the bank in Hamburg. It was not until the Aryanization of Warburgs that he left with his wife for Stockholm. Shortly afterward Max left for the United States. Max intended to return but did not.

Fritz did. Within weeks he was back in Hamburg for what he considered a vital meeting of the Jewish Hospitals Committee, of which he had long been president. He was arrested and thrown into prison. His Aryan friends, led by Christian Niemeyer, agitated vigorously for his release. Whether this agitation persuaded the Nazis to release him, or whether he actually escaped, seems uncertain.

Family tradition has it that a friendly warder left the door of his cell unlocked and that he walked out to freedom. He was, in any event, back in Stockholm before the end of the year.

After the war Fritz and Anna did not return to Germany but lived on in Sweden in semi-retirement. In 1962 Fritz went for the first time to Israel. There his two children were living on a kibbutz—they were the first Warburgs to take Israeli nationality. He died there—in that same year. He was the last of the five sons of Moritz and Charlotte.

Of all the sons Fritz had perhaps the least distinguished career. He was also the least assimilated. His children emigrated to Israel, the first members of the Warburg clan to do so. Fritz remained in Germany until it was almost too late, not because he felt himself first and foremost a German but out of loyalty to his brother Max. He had no conflict about whether to be German or Jewish and he had no urge to amass wealth or power. To that extent he stands apart from the mainstream of Warburg aspirations. It is fitting that this shadowy, much loved character, should die and be buried in Israel, precisely because it is so inappropriate for any of his banker brothers.

❧ CHAPTER TWELVE

Aby and the Warburg Institute *1866–1929*

IN MANY families there is one child who develops in ways utterly different from his siblings. Such was Moritz's and Charlotte's eldest son, Aby M. Warburg. The last of the five brothers to be discussed in this book, he stands apart from them all.

Born in 1866, he was struck by typhoid at the age of six, and was always a delicate child. The others were all very healthy. His mother's near-fatal illness in 1874 profoundly affected him, while his brothers and sisters were perhaps too young to be seriously touched by it. Though the oldest, he was spoiled by his parents, while the others, though much loved, were also much disciplined. Treated as the baby of the family, at the age of thirteen he decided to break completely from the family pattern. Finally, he was the only brother to marry a Gentile, and the first Warburg ever to do so.

While still in high school, Aby rebelled against the strict Jewish ritualism at home. He declared he wished to study the history of art. His decision provoked much opposition in the family, but Aby persisted, even taking an extra year of tutoring in the classics, in order to enter the University of Bonn.

In 1897 Aby visited the United States—in particular the Pueblo Indians. In that same year he traveled to Scandinavia, England,

[*126*]

and Florence, where he settled with his new (Gentile) wife, Mary.

Throughout this period, beginning with his university thesis, Aby was writing and publishing. While in Florence his reputation grew to such an extent that he was offered professorships at several universities. He invariably refused them. (The only professorship he accepted was that offered by the Hamburg Senate in 1912, and it was an honorific post, entailing no specific tasks.)

Always he shunned official posts and all that officialdom implied. He knew that his volatile temperament was totally alien to bureaucracy and all that it implied. Nonetheless one other offer may have tempted him. The Prussian minister of education asked him to become director of the Art Historical Institute at the prestigious University of Leipzig, but when he discovered that his main duty would be to spy on the existing and flashy professor of the history of art, whom the minister wanted to sack, he refused indignantly. He refused again when the same minister offered him the chair of art history at Halle.

Before then, like a homing pigeon, Aby had returned to his native city. There his fame as a teacher spread rapidly among the young. Students flocked to him. In 1909 his lectures on the Renaissance drew crowded audiences.

World War I dismayed him. He was bitterly critical of his country, attacking its leaders for their utter disregard for international law. He regarded Germany's defeat as no more than she deserved. He could never subscribe to the doctrine "My country right or wrong." He was no patriot but a scholar who believed scholarship should not recognize political boundaries.

It was partly the strain of wartime life that led to his mental collapse and withdrawal to an insane asylum in 1920—but only partly. There had always been a deep strain of pessimism and inadequacy in his personality. He himself had long been aware of the danger.

Years before, he had noted: "Two days out of the carnival of my life—one merry, then fever attack, inclination to day-dreaming,

Month of Torment, despairing anxiety about work which still has to be done."

In 1920 the shadows in his life seemed finally to have prevailed. Few thought he would ever emerge from his sanatorium near the Swiss border.

His favorite niece Gisela described a visit she paid him, accompanied by her father Max, when she was nine years old:

Aby was tortured by a persecution mania, and at one point he indicated a warder, saying, "Here is the man who poisons me every night."

He was carrying all his personal belongings in his pockets, convinced that otherwise they would be stolen.

But the evening after the visit he telephoned the girl's mother: "Tell Gisela that all I say is not the Truth." For a moment the darkness had lifted a little.

After four years Aby recovered completely and returned to the world of sanity. He returned, in his own mind, in triumph. He had won the final victory over the forces of evil. In one letter he even signed himself "Warburg *Redux.*"

"The Warburg of the twenties was decisive, even authoritarian, surrounded by followers and assistants. The little man with the black moustache, Aby, one square meter high, developed into a charismatic figure." [1]

In the next five years his energy was prodigious, and it was expended mainly on the private institute for the study of classical learning he had set up in 1905. Its full title was the Kulturwissens-chaftliche Bibliothek Warburg, but it was usually referred to as the Warburg Institute.

The idea for the institute was a product of Aby's experience as a university student. He had been struck by the difficulties of research due to compartmentalization. In their search for knowledge stu-

[1] Gertrude Bing, "Tribute to Aby Warburg," speech given at Hamburg University on Oct. 31, 1958.

dents were required to move from one specialized library to another.

Aby determined, in the words of his wife, "to give the students a library uniting the various branches of the history of civilization where he could wander from shelf to shelf."

It was a labor of Hercules. It required the frequent financial assistance not only of his brother Max, who had promised as a child to help Aby buy books if Max could run the firm, but of all his family, whose contribution to the achievement should not be forgotten. The development of the library needed constant reorganization to match each advance in Aby's thoughts, each new idea about the interrelation of facts.

It overspilled its original Hamburg home on Heilwigstrasse, and an adjoining house had to be purchased and adapted. Students flocked to it, as did teachers such as Ernst Cassirer, G. Pauli, and Erwin Panofsky to do their own research and to listen to Aby. It became, at least until the founding of Hamburg University, the center of the city's cultural life. By 1929 the Warburg Institute had published twelve volumes of *Studies* based on the research undertaken within its walls and housed forty thousand volumes. There had been a suggestion during his stay in the sanitorium that the library should be rehoused in a big public building in the center of Hamburg. On Aby's return he rejected this out of hand; it must at all costs retain its private and personal nature.

In 1929 this man of unique gifts died. His life displayed a crisscross pattern of depression and success, but his writing and his institute continue to exert great influence.

One of the curious aspects of Aby's career as a scholar and historian of art was his preservation of literally everything he wrote. His collected works contained everything from fully rounded essays to scraps of paper that are little more than rough drafts of a theory he might later have totally abandoned.

Published in Germany in 1932 they are still unavailable in translation. One result, according to his assistant, the late Gertrude

Bing, is that "even his posthumous fame comes more from hearsay than from a knowledge of his writings, and he is one of those authors whose fortune it is, in Lessing's words, to be more often praised than read."

Much of what he wrote is "unreadable" in the ordinary sense, because he wrote primarily to clarify his own thoughts. It was in transmitting them verbally that he triumphed.

His theories have been the subject of much controversy, raging around their originality as well as their content. It is obviously impossible to do justice to his life's work in this space. Yet Aby cannot be understood without some reference to what he wrote and thought.

With a work of art *per se* he was little concerned. It was a work of art's relation to the past, indeed to the whole history of man's development in thought and act that concerned him. Specifically, he was concerned time and again with the relationship of classical antiquity to High Renaissance art.

He did not claim to rediscover classical antiquity by himself. In this sphere he acknowledged a great debt to Karl Burckhardt. But it is claimed for him by his followers that it was he who undermined the crucial and long-held idea of classical "calm."

A constant theme of his writing was: What does the classical heritage mean for Western man? According to Professor E. H. Gombrich, Aby believed that the history of art had nothing to do with the abstract development of style, but with human beings who are faced with decisions and who consult the present and the past for advice.[2]

Aby's wife, who became his assistant in the library he formed, claimed after his death that his approach to art and the history of art had always been psychological and that his interest had never been in the arts as such, but only as their study helped to an understanding of the expressions of the mind.

[2] E. H. Gombrich, *Aby M. Warburg* (London, 1970).

The town of Warburg today. *Gerhard Stalling AG–Wirtshchaftsverlag*

Mr. and Mrs. Felix M. Warburg in 1899. *Culver Pictures*

Max Warburg about 1920. *Culver Pictures*

Paul M. Warburg (center) receiving an honorary degree of Doctor of Laws from Occidental College of Los Angeles in 1931. (left: Dr. R. D. Bird, President of Occidental; right: Dr. John Parke Young, Professor of Economics at Occidental.) *Wide World Photos*

Aby Warburg about 1925. *The Warburg Institute*

Mrs. Felix M. Warburg around 1930. *Foyer Photos*

Felix M. Warburg around 1930. *Culver Pictures*

Felix M. Warburg's New York City Residence at 1109 Fifth Avenue. *The Jewish Museum*

Sir Siegmund Warburg. *Lotte Meitner–Graf*

James P. Warburg (right) with former governor James M. Cox of Ohio, Vice-chairman of the American delegation to the World Economic Conference to be held in London, as they sailed from New York June 2, 1933 aboard the liner Olympic. *Wide World Photos*

Gerald Warburg in 1946.
Culver Pictures

Professor Otto H. Warburg
in 1931. *Culver Pictures*

Mr. and Mrs. Fredric John Warburg. *Angus McBean*

In this search for a synthesis of art and life Aby roamed far and wide in the field of art scholarship. He wrote about Botticelli's mythologies, Burgundian tapestries, Memling's portraits, Florentine engravings, German calendars, the business correspondence between the Medici and their agents abroad, controversies between Reformers and Counter-Reformers, Italian grand opera, court festivals, and quack medicines. He delved deep into the science of astrology.

Occasionally in his lectures he could be bewilderingly verbose, or simply pedantic, according to your point of view. One of his nephews recalls a five-hour lecture on the subject of why the king of England sat in the position of Neptune on the British pound note: "My recollection is that the last hour of the lecture consisted almost entirely of verbs." However, if often he led his students and his readers into mazes where it was very hard to find the exit, always he stimulated.

As a historian of art Aby is likely to remain a figure of controversy—perhaps that is the measure of greatness—because he forced people furiously to think.

The critic, Peter Burke has described it this way:

> Warburg had the gift of posing fruitful questions, of throwing out ideas which others could take up. Topics to which he devoted no more than a brief essay have turned into highly organized areas of research. . . . Later historians have often returned to problems which he had studied, such as the meaning of Botticelli's *Primavera* or of Dürer's *Melancolia* or of the Valois tapestries. Like the classical tradition the Warburg tradition has been transformed in the course of being transmitted. . . . The formation of this tradition obviously owed a good deal to Warburg's charismatic personality, but still more to the existence of his Institute.[3]

Gertrude Bing comments that his work "became so consequential because it was left as a fragment, with a fragment's power of testifying to a larger edifice and of challenging the imagination to supplement its details."

3 Peter Burke, "E. H. Gombrich's *Aby Warburg*," Oct. 21, 1971, *The Listener*.

What was he like, this man whom many consider to have been the most remarkable of all his tribe? He once described himself as *"Ebreo di sangue, Amburgese di cuore, d'anima Fiorentino"* ("A Jew by birth, a citizen of Hamburg at heart, a Florentine in spirit").

With the first and third definitions no one can quarrel. But that this man of deep culture should have his heart in Hamburg, should have chosen to live the last thirty years of his life in this city almost totally lacking in cultural traditions—until 1912 lacking even a university to its name—may seem at first strange. His wife explained that he deliberately chose to isolate himself from the bustling cultural centers of Göttingen, Heidelberg, and Berlin.

A more likely explanation is the tug of family ties. No matter that he had broken totally with his family's banking traditions. In Hamburg, where the Warburgs had lived for over a hundred years, he felt at home. He was part of that closely knit family, and almost every week he would write or talk to his brother Max about social, political, or economic matters. He delighted in the family circle, quite apart from the financial support it gave him. To regard him as a remote, ascetic scholar is totally to misunderstand him. He had a pixie sense of humor.

On one occasion, when his nephew Eric was called up for military service, he presented him with a revolver with a mother-of-pearl handle. For good measure he threw in an enormous scimitar—no soldier was properly equipped without a scimitar! Eric had to leave it in the care of a tram driver on his way to the barracks.

As a young man he loved dancing and danced with abandon. He was an ebullient student—if he had been attending a university in the 1960s he might well have been a leader of student protest.

He delighted in amateur theatricals and was a brilliant mimic. His compelling, luminous eyes could smile as well as brood. His friends thought that except for his small stature he might have made his fortune on the stage.

In 1928, a year before he died, a pear tree in his garden that had been given up for dead suddenly flowered. In one of his last letters he wrote, "Who will sing me the paean, the song of thanksgiving, in praise of the fruit tree that flowers so late?" Like the tree, he too had come back from the land of the dead.

There is a postscript to this brief account of Aby Warburg and his works. In the early 1930s the shadow of the Nazis was lengthening over the cultural activities of Germany. When they actually came to power in January, 1933, the activities of the Warburg Institute were reduced practically to nil. No lectures were allowed, and black marks were registered against students who made use of its facilities. It was, after all, not only cultural but Jewish in origin. It might well be altogether destroyed.

Aby's successor after his death, Dr. Fritz Saxl, decided that if possible the institute should be moved to a more friendly country. His decision was backed by Max Warburg, whose contacts abroad might prove helpful. The infamous Nazi book-burning incident [4] made a move seem imperative.

Some time was gained when the American consul general in Berlin announced publicly that part of the institute was American property (part of the money had after all been provided by Aby's American brothers). The mayor of Hamburg, who had the authority to allow the removal of the institute, was momentarily impressed.

Where, though, could the famous library go? The University of Leyden in Holland would take it but could not finance its transportation costs. The same yes-no answer came from Italy and the United States. Finally the plan to move came to the attention of two Englishmen, Professor Constable of the Courtauld Institute and Dr. Gibson of Guy's Hospital, who informed Sir Denison Ross, head of the London School of Oriental Studies. After a visit to

---

[4] On May 10, 1933, students staged a torchlight parade opposite the University of Berlin, featuring, as its climax, the burning of some twenty thousand books. They included works by Thomas Mann, Lion Feuchtwanger, Erich Maria Remarque, Albert Einstein, Jack London, Upton Sinclair, H. G. Wells, Sigmund Freud, André Gide, Emile Zola, and Marcel Proust.

Hamburg Sir Denison Ross returned enthusiastic and set up a committee headed by Lord Lee of Fareham. This group not only found temporary premises at Thames House on the Embankment in London but secured adequate financial support for three years from Samuel Courtauld and the Warburg family.

On October 28, 1933, Max Warburg received the following letter:

It has been brought to the notice of myself and certain of my friends who are also deeply interested in the history of art that the famous Warburg Library in Hamburg has, for the time being, practically ceased to function as a living institution. If this be so, it has occurred to me that it might be possible for this Library to be temporarily housed in London—say for a period of three years—so that the advantages and facilities which it offers to all students of art and culture might have an opportunity of continuing to be used and developed under the guidance of those who have for so long been connected with it.

In the event of its being possible for you to lend for such a period, I have much pleasure in informing you that—owing to the generous enthusiasm of a small group of friends who are interested in the history of art—I am in a position to offer you accommodation of a temporary character in the West End of London, which we shall be able to secure for this purpose.

We presume that—should this offer be accepted—it would enable you to continue the work of the Library and its development as in the past.

Yours sincerely,
Lee of Fareham

The letter was a lifeline. It was also the first example of the transactions subsequently known as Lend-Lease—something for nothing, payment deferred.

But would the move be sanctioned? For weeks the Hamburg government debated. Then to the great credit of the city the "ayes" had it. A face-saving formula was devised. The transfer to England would not be sanctioned, it would simply be ignored. The German press would not mention it, there must be no publicity in the British press adverse to the regime, and it would help matters if the institute would donate to the authorities two thousand volumes relating to World War I. Rarely can a forced donation have been so willingly given.

The move began. It involved sixty thousand books, thousands of slides and photographs, and a large amount of furniture. Five hundred and thirty boxes in all were loaded onto two steamers. On December 12, 1933, they started to move slowly down the Elbe. That same afternoon Aby's widow served tea to the packers in the now bare elliptical room in the library that had been built shortly before his death. Each man, specially picked, was a staunch anti-Nazi.

A fortnight later, responsibility for such transactions was transferred to Joseph Goebbels' propaganda ministry in Berlin. There can be little doubt what Dr. Goebbels would have decided.

The three years passed, and thanks to the generosity of Samuel Courtauld, the library's life in London was extended to a further seven, passed in the Imperial Institute buildings loaned to the Warburg Institute by the University of London. In 1944 the destiny of Aby's great library was finally decided. It was incorporated into the University of London and given premises in Woburn Square. A contributory factor to this decision was that of the books in the library one in every ten was *not* possessed by the British Museum.

Since Aby's day the library has grown greatly in size and scope, but under the directorship of his prize pupil and colleague Fritz Saxl, and his successor Professor E. H. Gombrich, Aby's original scheme has been preserved.

Among its 190,000 volumes can be found sections on psychology, anthropology, the history of music and the stage, festivals and pageantry, magic and science, printing and illustration, iconography, early Christian and Byzantine art, tattooing, and histories of every important medieval Italian city. In the opinion of Professor Gombrich the collection deals with much more than the history of art. It is a repository for the whole history of ideas.

⚜ CHAPTER THIRTEEN

Otto: The Nobel
Prize Winner *1883–1970*

PROFESSOR Aby M. Warburg, despite his eccentricities, was still a member of the main stem of the family tree. The son of Moritz and Charlotte, the grandson of Sara, he was the uncle or close cousin of those who are dominant in the Warburg family today.

Professor Otto Warburg, though only a remote cousin, perhaps resembles Aby more closely than any of his other relatives. He was aware of his idiosyncratic nature. He often used to say he admired England over all other countries, because "the English tolerate headstrong and eccentric people."

Professor Otto Warburg was certainly headstrong. Just before his death in 1970 the author of this book requested an interview. Otto immediately sent off to Max Warburg's son, Eric, a letter of complaint:

The relationship between my family and the Hamburg branch of the Warburg family is so distant that it cannot really be regarded as a relationship at all. This apart, neither family has ever had social or business dealings with each other. . . . I myself met you and your parents in Hamburg in 1933 when I visited you there. But this small beginning of an acquaintanceship soon ended when your family left Germany, while I remained like many hundreds of thousands of artists, scholars and members of great Prussian families who, racially speaking, were in the same situation as I. So why now on paper, in a book, should an intimate connection be simulated which has never existed and does not exist today? My wish is that my family should be kept out of the book.

Otto Warburg was indeed a far cry—not only by ancestry—from the mainstream of the Warburgs. They were all more or less cosmopolitan in that they had interests outside their careers. Otto decidedly did not. His one interest in life was the study of biochemistry. Of all the Warburg clan he was the most blinkered to the outside world.

Professors Aby and Otto shared two characteristics that set them apart from the rest of the family. They were, to put it mildly, lax in their pursuit of wealth, and they showed no desire to assimilate with the Gentile world around them.

Born in 1883, Otto was trained in chemistry and then in medicine, obtaining his doctorate in the former at Berlin in 1906 and in the latter at Heidelberg in 1911.

In 1913 he was appointed to a permanent research post in the Kaiser Wilhelm Gesellschaft (in 1948 renamed the Max Planck Institute). Thereafter, apart from a period of war service from 1914 to 1918, he devoted his entire life to the pursuit of science. In 1931 the Rockefeller Foundation built for him an entirely new institute, the Kaiser Wilhelm Institut für Zellenphysiologie. He was still working there at his death nearly forty years later.

In the same year, 1931, he was awarded the Nobel prize for medicine. The citation read in part: "for the discovery of the catalytic role of iron phorphyrins in biological oxydation." [1]

Very briefly, he maintained that cancer, contrary to the then prevalent opinion, could at an early stage be easily diagnosed and cured, that it was caused by fermentation taking the place of

[1] Biographical Memoirs of the Fellows of the Royal Society, ed. H. A. Krebs, Vol. 18, Nov., 1972. Otto was made a foreign member of the society in 1934.

breathing in the human cells, and that it was absent in primitive peoples who knew nothing of artificial foodstuffs. He attacked the use of artificial coloring to make food more tempting, of "faked" fruit juices whose base was largely composed of mineral substances. He persuaded the German government to require that all such artificial aids should be specified on the bottles concerned.

His unique distinction was to be the first to combine the methods of classical organic chemistry with those of radiation physics. As early as 1927 he had been considered for a Nobel prize. After winning it in 1931, he was considered again in 1944 for his further research, but by that time Adolf Hitler had decreed that no German must accept it. Nevertheless, Otto's fame was so great that Hitler, though he restricted his activities, dared not touch this particular Jew. He remained at his institute throughout the war.

Though Otto always refused to be a professional teacher he kept the doors of his institute in the Salem suburb of Berlin open to students or fellow chemists. When he wished, he could exercise great charm, provided his audience accepted his importance.

He could also be the reverse. He was a doughty, sarcastic, even vindictive fighter for his beliefs and his reputation. Sarcasm broke out in a letter to that remote cousin Eric after the war: "Herr X, who has got a Nobel Prize, started his career with me, beginning with a thesis in 1934. In fact, three of my pupils have got Nobel Prizes. Why don't *you* try to write a thesis?"

The doughty, vindictive fighter appeared in a conference of Nobel prize winners at Lindau, Switzerland in 1966, when he attacked his younger colleagues as false prophets "who struggle against the true perceptions of science," accusing them of bearing indirect responsibility for the deaths from cancer of millions of human beings. He was a stormy petrel who grew even stormier as his life drew to its end.

In his private life he remained solitary. He never married and had a passion for dogs and horses. The former made a visit to him at his house, which adjoined the institute, a perilous undertaking.

He loathed journeys by rail or car. When, each spring, he visited his country property on Rügen Island off the Baltic coast, he went on horseback, a full day's journey. He frequently declared his detestation of all newspapers, above all *The Times*, in which, he once maintained to Eric, it was impossible to find one's way. Soon afterward Eric sent him a sample copy, whereupon he became a regular subscriber, spending an hour a day for the rest of his life in reading it.

His personal life was almost entirely controlled by one man. His name was Heiss. Heiss had been Otto's orderly in World War I. He became first butler, then administrator of Otto's estate, and finally, at least where finance was concerned, his alter ego.

Once, on one of Eric's visits, Otto asked Eric whether he should sell his shares in the Deutsche Bank. Heiss, who was serving the meal, intervened at once. He must wait until the next dividends were paid, he said.

He was, Eric says now, absolutely right, adding, with a touch of hyperbole, "at least as well versed as our stock market department at the bank."

From this man, an unlettered soldier, Otto received unstinting devotion. To this man, the Nobel prize winner gave an affection he accorded to no one else.

Otto's institute was partly funded by the Rockefeller Foundation in America. An initial 3 million marks to help establish it was followed by an annual subsidy of 130,000 marks for research. After the Nazis came to power, the Rockefeller Foundation suggested that Otto and his institute escape to a more democratic climate. Otto refused. He was wedded to Salem and to the laboratory assistants he had trained. What was happening in the outside world was no concern of his.

So, unlike that other Warburg institution, Aby's library, Otto's institute stayed put, and the Rockefeller subsidy ceased.

THE WARBURGS

One of Eric Warburg's sisters, Anita, emigrated to England shortly after the Rockefeller funds had stopped. Eric gave her funds on which Otto could draw for the purchase of needed books from London. Otto quickly drew on $75 of this money, not for books, but because as he later told Eric, "One can't get decent riding breeches and boots in Germany any longer."

This eccentric genius sat it out in Germany through the entire period of Nazi rule, in peace and in war. When the Russians broke through on the Eastern front he was at his country house on the island of Rügen.

To the first Russian he encountered, he is alleged to have said, "Do you know who I am? The famous Nobel prize winner, Professor Otto Warburg from Berlin."

His manner certainly impressed the Russians. Marshal Georgi Zhukov sent him as a gift two Caucasian horses and a car, plundering his estate was forbidden, and food parcels from overseas were allowed in. Later he was even invited to visit Russia, but having lived and remained unscalded in the frying pan of Hitler's dictatorship he had no desire to sample the fire of Stalinist Russia, and refused.

When he returned to Salem from his country house, the Americans took strict precautions to prevent him from being kidnapped. At the start of the Russian blockade of Berlin five years later, Otto was persuaded to go to America. The visit was not a success. He quarreled violently with leading professors in his field and was relieved to return to Salem.

In the last years of his life he bought a small property well to the west of Berlin—but not because it was farther away from that trouble spot. The reason, as he wrote to Eric, was that "the district is the most thinly populated in the whole of Germany." In his last letter to that cousin whose relationship he appeared to despise, he wrote: "I shall get the third Nobel Prize for us, because in one or two years we shall have resolved the problem of cancer."

He died before achieving this aim, but no one in recent times has done so much to make a solution possible.

Professor Sir Henry Krebs, emeritus professor of biochemistry at Oxford University, has described Professor Otto as belonging "to the small band of real architects of modern biology" and "a supreme master of the art of experimentation."

CHAPTER FOURTEEN

Jimmy: Politician or Pamphleteer? *1896–1969*

FOUR—some would say all—of the sons of Moritz and Charlotte possessed qualities of character and inspiration that raised them above the ordinary run of men. In their different ways, Aby, Max, Paul, and Felix would have been remarkable at any time and in any place.

In the next Warburg generation this could be said of only two members of the family, Siegmund and James P., and of these two James P. (known throughout the Anglo-American world as "Jimmy") was the most protean. Jimmy, the only son of Paul, died in 1969 at the age of seventy-two after a lifetime of activities more manifold than those of any other Warburg dead or alive.

It can be said of him that, starting out as virtually a playboy, he ended up a man whose liberal principles and actions won the respect and affection of two American presidents and whose abilities carried him on several occasions to the threshold of high political office. His thirty books include *The Money Muddle*, which became a classic of its kind. If he had defects they seem in retrospect almost as appealing as his virtues.

The children of Paul and of Felix Warburg were the first members of the family to approach complete assimilation. Their fathers had traveled a long way along that road, but their back-grounds and education were German and Jewish.

Jimmy was only eleven when his father settled permanently in the United States. He was sent, like his cousins, the children of Felix, to Middlesex, a Unitarian school in Concord, Massachusetts, and from there, like many other alumni, to Harvard. It was all very Waspish.

His education was American and Gentile, and at both school and university he enjoyed himself. His loyalties were totally American, and in due course he became a member of the American "Establishment."

A handful of anti-Semitic strongholds denied him admittance. He was never asked, for example, to become a member of the famous Century Club of New York. (It had previously rejected the candidature of Alfred Knopf, one of the most celebrated of American publishers, on the grounds of race.)

Jimmy was well aware that anti-Semitism was still pervasive in the United States as it was in German and British life. Assimilation could never be total so long as anti-Semitism continued to exist.

In a privately printed little book of advice to his children, he warned that they would grow up in a country "in which, because you are half-Jewish, not all the doors will be open to you."

He told them of the shock he had felt as a little boy in Hamburg when he found he was something called a Jew, which was different both from his English nanny and the Kaiser. How, after he went to school in America, he decided that he must understand what the Jewish religion was all about and studied under his uncle Felix's favorite rabbi, Judah Magnes, and how he came to reject what the rabbi had taught him:

> My faith is very simple. I believe in God and in his having created man as a creature endowed with reason and with the capacity gradually to perfect himself in God's image. I believe in the Golden Rule and the brotherhood of man. I believe that man was put on this earth for a higher purpose than to trample himself in the mire of fratricidal war.

Jimmy in fact could not bring himself to entirely accept either the Jewish faith or any of the different brands of organized Christianity. His Judaism gave way to a form of affirmative agnosticism. He dubbed it, "Jeffersonian deism."

What is certain is that he loathed intolerance of any kind:

So long as there is any discrimination by Christians against Jews [he told his children], such as keeping them out of clubs, summer resorts and certain residential districts, I would rather be a Jew than a member of the Christian majority. I would rather be discriminated against by reason of race and religion than be guilty of such discrimination.

Jimmy had the force of character to ignore these racial pinpricks. He was an American citizen, convinced of America's mission in the world in a way that neither his immigrant father nor his uncle Felix could ever quite be. For most of his life he was a liberal Democrat, and for all his apparent inconsistencies, his sudden changes of stance, Jimmy was devoted to the promotion of American ideals and ideas. He valued the Jewish cultural inheritance, so strikingly emphasized in the careers of Felix's children, but he was uninterested in Judaism as such. He never visited the new State of Israel. He never became involved in the passionate Zionist–non-Zionist controversies that so agitated his uncle Felix and to a lesser extent Felix's children. For him the United States, not Israel, was "God's own Country."

As a young man Jimmy the protean would try his hand at anything. At Harvard it was sports. In fact he broke a track record and his feelings were hurt when after he had boasted about it to his cousin Fredrick he was told that half a hurricane had been blowing at his back.

Like most protean men Jimmy had a good deal of vanity in his makeup. In the words of his closest friend, the late Joseph Barnes, he wanted not only to excel in everything but also to be praised for his successes.

In his apprentice days, before he became a full-fledged financier, he worked for a while as a junior clerk in the First National Bank in Boston and while there wrote a pamphlet on the sheep-raising industry, though his acquaintance with these animals was limited.

As the oldest male member of the thirteenth generation of a banking family, Jimmy expected to enter Kuhn, Loeb & Co., whose major business was financing railroads. He decided he should learn first-hand how a railroad operated, and for six months worked for the Baltimore & Ohio Railroad.

One day Jimmy was assigned as temporary foreman to a rough gang that included a particularly tough Irishman. Jimmy delivered a "pep" talk to the gang that was answered by a stream of insults from this worker. He decided there was only one way to respond, and launched his attack. Having been twice knocked down, Jimmy changed his tactics and aimed a blow at what Sir Winston Churchill might have called the "soft under-belly." Luckily for Jimmy, the Irishman was not only a bruiser but a boozer. He fell groaning to the ground. From then on they regularly sent each other Christmas cards.

In what may be called his playboy guise, he wrote under the pseudonym Paul James the lyrics of *Fine and Dandy*, a musical comedy backed by himself and two millionaires, Marshall Field and Averell Harriman. The show was a hit, and ran for well over a year.

The pseudonym was compulsory. It just would not have done for even a *junior* partner in Kuhn, Loeb to be associated publicly with the show-biz world of Broadway. In the Wall Street offices the ghost of the straitlaced Jacob Schiff still presided.

By his midtwenties Jimmy had also joined his father's highly reputable International Acceptance Bank. Nonetheless, when he was in London, Jimmy frequented the famous, and to put it mildly, unorthodox Cavendish Hotel, presided over by the eccentric Rosa Lewis, ex-cook to King Edward VII.

It was initially as his father's deputy that he made his debut on the European financial stage. He had been deeply involved in the troubles that beset the family firm in Germany in 1930. As an indirect result of this involvement he played a leading part in a little-known negotiation, which, had it succeeded, would in Jimmy's view have cut one leg from under the Nazis' drive for power.

The failure of the Kreditanstalt in 1931 had set in train a series of events that threatened the collapse of the entire German financial edifice. It seemed to Jimmy vitally necessary to restore confidence in the future of the four biggest German joint stock banks, which controlled much of German industry. He proposed to his father that a number of American banks should join in converting their foreign assets in Germany into fresh capital with which to shore up the weakest of these banks. After all, the injection of American money into M. M. Warburg & Co. had, only a few months before, worked wonders in restoring confidence. Now, on a much larger scale, a fund of 50 million marks was provided, armed with which Jimmy, with his uncle Max (who at that time still had unrestricted entrée to the highest financial circles in Berlin), approached the chancellor, Heinrich Brüning.

Brüning welcomed the scheme unreservedly and sent them to see President Luther of the Reichsbank. The latter named the weakest of the banks, the Darmstädter Nationalbank, as the patient most in need of Jimmy's treatment.

So far so good. But early in the examination of the bank's books "Account X" raised its ugly head. On whether this represented a valid or worthless asset might depend the solvency of the bank, but all information was refused. In its place, a general assurance was given that the account was good. On this point, negotiations broke down, and Jimmy returned to New York.

Years later he discovered that "Account X" represented a loan to President Hindenburg's son Oscar. As an asset it was as worthless as was Oscar's character. But to have revealed this fact would have been to bring odium on the name of Hindenburg. Moreover, it was deemed impossible to approach the aging and ailing president on the matter. Hitler and his financial henchman Hjalmar Schacht had reason to be grateful to "Account X."

Jimmy was not a Warburg for nothing, and finance was in his blood. He succeeded his father as president of the International Acceptance Bank, and he sat on the board of the Union Pacific Railroad.

In 1937, Jimmy was "godfather" to the infant Polaroid Corporation, formed to exploit Edwin Land's newly invented light-polarizing plastic. It was Jimmy's investment of his own money that convinced the usually conservative Kuhn, Loeb board to participate in the underwriting of the preferred stock of the new company. After the shakiest of starts, due to the refusal of the automobile industry to use the material to cut down headlight glare, the Polaroid Corporation was to make a fortune both for Land and Jimmy, with the subsequent invention by Land of the revolutionary photographic process used in the Polaroid Land Camera.

A cancer operation in 1961 meant Jimmy had to spend much of his time in Florida. There he invested in real estate, building apartment houses at Deerfield Beach on the Florida coast, and having designed a remarkable restaurant in the form of an indoor aboretum with a stream running through it, and a grotto underneath.

It was as an expert on finance that at the age of thirty-six he first caught the eye of President Franklin D. Roosevelt.

From that moment on, Jimmy Warburg's main preoccupation was public affairs. He was the first Warburg to tread that road, and so far has had no successor.

Franklin D. Roosevelt was elected President of the United States in November, 1932. Roosevelt's son James was already living in a house on Felix Warburg's White Plains estate, where he had become a close friend of Jimmy. Another friend of the young Roosevelt was Professor Raymond Moley, one of Franklin Roosevelt's closest advisers and leader of the President's unofficial brain trust. Moley and Jimmy were introduced to one another by James, and shortly afterward Moley took Jimmy to see the President. It was the beginning of an intense and stormy relationship.

Roosevelt inherited a financial situation that was close to chaos. The crash on Wall Street in 1929 had snowballed to such an extent that by March, 1933, every bank throughout the country had either closed its doors or was allowing only limited withdrawals. Jimmy was summoned by Moley to Washington and told to submit a plan whereby the banks could be reopened. His scheme, only partially put into effect, nonetheless led to the reopening of 90 percent of the nation's banks within a week.

Moley was impressed. So was the President. Rumors about young Warburg's future began to multiply. The parallel with his father's growing reputation nearly thirty years earlier was obvious.

Would he too become a governor of the Federal Reserve Board? *The New York Times* claimed that he was about to be appointed Under Secretary of the Treasury. The latter post was in fact offered to him.

But to accept would have under the rules governing acceptance of government office compelled him to sell—on the weakest possible market—his recently widowed mother's shares in one of the big banks, for in these shares Jimmy had a contingent interest. To have done so would have gravely depleted her funds.

His mother urged him to sell and take the post. He refused. But when the American delegation to the London Economic Conference sailed a few months later, President Roosevelt showed his continued regard for Jimmy by appointing him its financial adviser.

As he sailed across the Atlantic Jimmy may have felt he was on the threshold of international fame. If so, he was to be rapidly disillusioned. Of all the international conferences held between the wars, he was on his way to the least organized, and the most doomed to failure of them all. Its collapse left not even a whiff of tragedy behind it, only a momentary aroma of sad farce.

The chapter in his autobiography *The Long Road Home* [1] in

1 James P. Warburg, *The Long Road Home* (New York: Doubleday, 1964).

which Jimmy described this conference is appropriately called "Fiasco in London." Few of the delegations had any real idea of what they wanted, the American least of all.

Arthur Schlesinger, Jr., wrote in *The Coming of the New Deal:*

In London all was confusion. Delegates from sixty-six lands milled around the Geological Museum at Kensington, strolling in and out of committee-rooms, forming knots of conversation in the corridors, or retreating in despair to the seventy-foot bar on the lower floor to sip drinks of all nations. Of all the delegations none was more confused than the American.[2]

Presiding over the conference was the aging Socialist peacock, Ramsay MacDonald, prime minister of Britain's national government in nothing but name, already the prisoner of the Tories.

Leading the Americans was Secretary of State Cordell Hull, whom his President consistently bypassed. Both these men and their sixty-four counterparts were bound in their thinking by the internal monetary stresses of their own countries.

The American delegation comprised men of diametrically opposed views: hard-line old "gold-standard-at-any-price" economists were opposed by all-out inflationists. Somewhere in the middle stood Jimmy Warburg, convinced that it was imperative to finally jettison the old rigid gold standard, and equally convinced that it must be replaced in due course by something similar.

Paramount was the need for a temporary currency truce, if the wider economic issues were to be successfully tackled. To this end, Jimmy had already formulated back in Washington a directive to the American delegation that Roosevelt, with the deviousness that was to become one of the most successful and least admirable features of his administrations, had neither approved nor rejected. To this end too, Jimmy worked for and succeeded in getting the

---

[2] Arthur Schlesinger, *The Coming of the New Deal* (New York: Houghton Mifflin, 1958), p. 240.

British and French to agree to a formula for the temporary stabilization of the dollar, pound, and franc.

This formula was transmitted to Roosevelt with an urgent plea from Jimmy that without its acceptance "it would be practically impossible to assume a leading role in attempting to bring about a lasting economic peace."

A fortnight of presidential silence followed, rashly assumed by Jimmy to indicate assent. Finally he sent a follow-up message and received a bombshell in reply.

Roosevelt rejected any thought of a currency truce or any idea of an eventual return to a reformed version of the gold standard. Jimmy resigned.

Not long after, amid a welter of mutual recriminations in which Roosevelt featured as the main villain, the conference broke up in futile disarray.

Jimmy's resignation led to no immediate breach with the President. On his return to America he was frequently called into consultation at the White House. His advice, it must be admitted, was usually rejected. But he was moving farther away from Roosevelt's New Deal policies and back into the arms of his orthodox Wall Street colleagues, even though the latter continued to regard him with suspicion. For a man to have any dealing at all with "that man in the White House" amounted in the eyes of the men of Wall Street—Republicans almost to a man—to little short of treachery.

In 1934 Jimmy's first book, *The Money Muddle*,[3] was published. He sent a complimentary copy to Roosevelt. The letter accompanying it and the President's reply are equally revealing. Jimmy wrote:

> There will be a general predisposition to regard the book as hostile to the New Deal. It is my hope that anyone who reads it through will find that such is far from being the case. It is my hope—perhaps unjustified—that I may contribute in some small measure towards stilling some of the extreme clamor from what Ray Moley once called "the brainless left and the imaginationless right."

3 New York: Knopf, 1934.

Thus Jimmy Warburg assumed his role as the man of the center in public. Increasingly it became his political stance.

Roosevelt replied:

Some day I hope you will bring out a second edition—but will you let an old friend make a special request of you before you do it? Please get yourself an obviously secondhand Ford car; put on your oldest clothes and start west for the Pacific coast, undertaking beforehand not to speak on the entire trip with any banker or business executive (except gas stand owners) and to put up at no hotel where you have to pay more than $1.50 a night.

Here is the American aristocrat with his lifelong hatred of the big-business community very thinly disguised.

He concluded the letter: "After the above insulting 'advice to a young man'—do nevertheless run down and see me some day." [4]

Roosevelt's lifelong hatred of the business world never included, despite the events of the ensuing years, the brilliant young banker-politician from Bydale, Connecticut.

Jimmy had first publicly attacked the administration's monetary policies soon after his return from the London Economic Conference. He did so again in his second book, *It's Up to Us*,[5] in which he first adumbrated his fears of the new federal powers the President was increasingly accumulating. Roosevelt proved remarkably tolerant of his former protégé's forays, regarding him as an irritating but basically friendly "Wasp" (though not a white Anglo-Saxon protestant one), but in 1936 a breach occurred that was never fully mended. Jimmy, its initiator, later regarded it as the biggest mistake of his life.

In the elections of 1936 Jimmy chose to throw his weight behind the Republican party. He had come to the totally erroneous conclusion that the massive new powers which Roosevelt was securing for the federal government spelled dictatorship, and dictatorship meant Hitler and Mussolini.

[4] James P. Warburg, *The Long Road Home*, p. 157.
[5] New York: Knopf, 1935.

In *Hell Bent for Election*,[6] first serialized in 1935, he painted a picture of a President hungry for power and popular acclaim. It was meat and drink for the Republicans, who distributed a million copies of the book throughout the country.

Jimmy himself formally joined the Republican party, to find himself marching under banners which had been anathema to him all his life. He chose to campaign in the primaries for Colonel Frank Knox, whom he considered the most enlightened of the Republican candidates, though his newspaper the *Chicago Daily News* was not noted for its liberal tendencies. He was alarmed when Alfred Landon was chosen as the candidate. When Landon showed his narrow nationalist outlook by denouncing the recently passed Reciprocal Trade Agreements Jimmy was appalled. To Jimmy the agreements constituted one of the Roosevelt administration's finest achievements.

In the end Jimmy felt he couldn't vote for such a leader. With considerable courage he made public what amounted to a double apostasy in an open letter to Secretary of State Cordell Hull, telling him that he would vote Democratic.

No one takes kindly to public figures who change sides. Despite a subsequent reconciliation with Roosevelt, which showed in full measure the President's generosity of spirit, it is probable that by his fluctuations in 1936 Jimmy Warburg lost forever the chance of attaining high office.

In the year that followed the election, Jimmy's almost total preoccupation was with the European situation. He had first sensed the reality of the Nazi menace when he visited his uncle Max in Hamburg after the collapse of his hopes at the London Economic Conference in 1933. At that time he had pleaded in vain with his uncle to go while the going was still good. Further visits to Europe strengthened his conviction of impending disaster. He was the first

6 New York: Knopf, 1936.

American publicly to advocate (in *Our War and Our Peace* [7]) that the United States should regard any attack on the Western democracies as an attack on itself. This was before the Nazi move on Poland.

More pragmatically, in December, 1940, when Britain stood alone against the Germans, he wrote *The New York Times* that if American law prevented the lending of money to the beleaguered island, America must *give* it.

Roosevelt's Lend-Lease Act of March, 1941, did not satisfy him. Shortly afterward, he was one of the small group who founded the Fight for Freedom Committee, pledged to all-out intervention on behalf of Britain.

In a passionate radio speech launching this committee in April, 1941, he attacked the "America Firsters" who were maintaining that Hitler had already won, that it was too late to do anything. Together with Herbert Agar, the journalist,[8] he became the chief champion of beleaguered Britain. At a mass rally at Madison Square Garden he attacked the archisolationist and former national hero, Colonel Charles Lindbergh:

> Colonel Lindbergh wants a "practical plan" to defeat Hitler. . . . As to how this is done I refer Colonel Lindbergh to the Royal Air Force, to John Paul Jones or Commodore Perry, or for that matter to the Lindbergh of 1927 who flew across the ocean. The question of whether it is too late is not a question for experts. That is a question for us, the ordinary citizens of America, just as it is a question for the people of Britain, of Greece, of China—yes, and even the people of the conquered countries. For this is nothing more than a question of faith, of courage, and of determination.
>
> We of the Fight for Freedom Committee say it is not too late.

[7] New York: Farrar & Rinehart, 1941.

[8] Herbert Agar's many journalistic appointments in the United States included the editorship of the *Louisville Courier-Journal* (1939–42). He served in the U.S. Navy in both world wars. He was special assistant to the American ambassador in London from 1942 to 1946. His books include *Abraham Lincoln, A Time for Greatness,* and *The Perils of Democracy.*

THE WARBURGS

We say that our only danger of "humiliation and defeat" lies in the possibility of our being crushed between the upper and the nether millstones of defeatism and complacency.

If we allow ourselves to be confused by the Lindberghs, the Wheelers, the Clarks, and the Nyes—if we allow our courage to be undermined, our faith to be shaken, our determined action to be delayed—then indeed we may face the certainty of humiliation and the danger of deserved defeat.

But, if we listen to our consciences, we know what it is that we must do. We know that there can be no compromise. We know that as free men we must fight now or later.

And, if we listen to our common sense, we know that if we fight now, with Britain and her Allies to help us, our chances of victory are far better than if we wait until perhaps we shall have to fight alone.

And, finally, if we listen to the voice of our inner faith, we know that nothing so foul as this brutal beast, which has launched itself upon the world, can forever remain triumphant—that even though some may die fighting, there will be others and still others willing to die for freedom rather than live as slaves, until eventually the beast is slain.

Was it too late for Washington and his ragged soldiers in that grim winter at Valley Forge?

Was it too late for Nelson at Trafalgar, or for Wellington at Waterloo?

Was it too late for Britain last summer, when France fell?

A strange thing has happened to a few good Americans like Colonel Lindbergh—a man of undoubted courage, a man who did not fear to set out alone against heavy odds—but who now preaches the doctrine of defeat—who urges us to go home before the game is over because our side is behind in the early innings.

Perhaps for Colonel Lindbergh, and others like him, the game is over.

If, throughout history, men had been willing to fight only when the percentage was in their favor, when victory seemed theirs for the taking, where would civilization be today?

Where would it be tomorrow if America were to follow the advice of those who falsely call themselves the America First Committee—who would have us betray our own best hope of defense by holding back our shipments of material aid to Britain—who would have us betray our souls by holding back our bodies from danger—until the day when neither the sacrifice of our bodies nor of our souls will serve to avert disaster?

Jimmy: Politician or Pamphleteer? 1896–1969

If you believe in thinking of America first, of America first, and of
yourself last—if you believe in such a thing as a just cause for which no
sacrifice is too great—then join us, who say to you:

This is *our* Fight for Freedom. This is no "foreign war," nor is it a fight
to save any other nation. It is our fight—for us to win, or for us to lose. The
longer we wait the harder will be our battle.

It was of course the Japanese, not Jimmy Warburg or Herbert
Agar, who forced the United States into war, but the two men had
done much to assist the President's more subtle efforts to soften up
the isolationist ranks to unite the nation when the test came.

In the same month that President Roosevelt and Prime Minister Winston Churchill proclaimed the Four Freedoms at their
Atlantic Charter meeting, August, 1941, Jimmy was appointed
special assistant to Colonel William Donovan, Roosevelt's coordinator of information. It marked his return to the official fold.

At the outbreak of war he joined the Office of War Information, headed by Elmer Davis, with Robert E. Sherwood, the dra-
matist, as chief of its overseas branch. Jimmy was placed in charge of
propaganda to German-occupied Europe. His headquarters was
London, and his main task to coordinate British and American
propaganda warfare.

London had long been a second home to him, ever since the
days of Rosa Lewis and the Cavendish Hotel. Now he was fighting
for a cause he had long advocated. He was surrounded by fellow
Anglophiles, headed by the ambassador, John G. Winant (Herbert
Agar was his special assistant), and Averell Harriman, the President's unofficial troubleshooter, and was in close touch with Britain's chief war planners.

His lot in life was cast again in pleasant places, the future once
again beckoned brightly, as it had eight years earlier, on the eve of
the London Economic Conference.

Jimmy worked hard and happily for nearly two years. Then, in
July, 1943, at the time of Benito Mussolini's arrest by the Fascist
grand council and his forced resignation, Jimmy found himself in

trouble. Then in New York, Jimmy authorized and under an assumed name delivered a radio speech that in a general condemnation of fascism criticized King Umberto of Italy and his prime minister, Marshal Pietro Badoglio.

He had justification for the broadcast. The joint Anglo-American chiefs of staff had earlier issued a directive that the Italian royal family should be included in any condemnation of the Fascist regime, and earlier, before the Allied invasion of Italy, General Dwight D. Eisenhower had said the same thing. The Office of War Information had been told "not to spare the House of Savoy for its support of Fascism." [8]

Unknown, however, to Jimmy, the British at that time were far more fearful of communism than the Americans and were pointedly excluding the House of Savoy from their gleeful announcement of Mussolini's downfall. A royal family, however suspect, might prove a bulwark of a kind against the Red menace, even though that menace was at the time a gallant ally.

For the time being, Roosevelt was inclined to follow the British line. The American press launched a violent attack on the Office of War Information. Arthur Krock wrote in *The New York Times* that the broadcast had "served the interests of the communists and endangered the lives of American soldiers." The President denounced the broadcast at a press conference, adding salt to Jimmy's wounds by stating that Robert Sherwood had not authorized it and was raising hell about it.

"This was not true," Jimmy wrote in *The Long Road Home*,[9] "but for reasons known only to himself, Sherwood neither corrected the President's misapprehension as to his own responsibility nor made it clear that the New York office had strictly followed directives."

Nonetheless, at a meeting of the Overseas Board of the OWI in Washington a week later, Jimmy thought he had received the full

[8] *The Long Road Home*, p. 202.
[9] p. 202.

support of both Sherwood and Milton D. Eisenhower, the President's special adviser. He let a further week pass and then set forth his views in a memorandum to Sherwood and Elmer Davis.

Our present attitude suggests that we do not want an anti-Fascist or anti-Nazi revolution [in the liberated territories] at all, that we are afraid of it and will not take the lead and give to it the backbone of our military power. Once this conception of our war aims takes root in the minds of the people of Europe, they will regard us not as liberators but as the agents of reactionary suppression. And if this happens, our armed forces are likely to encounter hostile populations who will actively support the enemy.

He exaggerated, but there was truth in his contention.

This should have been the end of the matter, but although Jimmy remained at his post for another six months, he had become the victim of a violent squabble between Sherwood and Elmer Davis.

As a method of destroying Sherwood's power, Davis conceived the idea of getting rid of his chief assistant. According to Jimmy, Sherwood weakly assented to his dismissal, and on February 5, 1944, Jimmy received a letter from Davis demanding his resignation: "My observation of your work for some months past has convinced me that your activity has on the whole tended to confusion in our operations. . . . Accordingly, I ask for your immediate resignation."

Jimmy's reply was brief and to the point:

In accordance with the request contained in your letter of February 5th, I hereby tender my resignation to take effect immediately, although I repudiate as false the general allegation as well as the specific example cited in your letter. What is more I believe that you know your statement to be false.

A few days later Jimmy wrote to the President, representing himself as a casualty "in a regrettable and unseemly squabble," but adding, "In a time like the present no one likes to sit on the sidelines, and light casualties frequently do return to battle. I hope

I may be one of those who do, and that you will take for granted my willingness to serve wherever and however I can." [10]

Roosevelt's answer was a masterpiece of double-talk:

Dear Jimmy, I want you to know how deeply I appreciate the fine spirit which prompts your letter of February 10th. Many thanks. I, too, regret your withdrawal from the public service. Bob [Sherwood] has told me of the high quality of your work and I know he too regrets the circumstances which impel you to the decision to leave. I am glad to have your assurance that I can take for granted your willingness to serve wherever and however you can.[11]

They were fair enough words, but they were never implemented. Jimmy was never again to hold a government post. His dismissal left a deep scar on his memory. His description of it in *The Long Road Home* is the only passage in the book where bitterness creeps in. Of Sherwood's part in the affair, he wrote, sadly: "It remains my sole experience of being let down by a friend." [12]

But was Jimmy wholly blameless, or was he the victim of his own temperament? He had shown his impetuosity in his precipitate resignation from the London Economic Conference, and in the presidential campaign of 1936 he had behaved with a maximum of folly. He cannot have been an easy man to work with—his interests were basically political, his abiding concern the international situation, but he was a maverick in his chosen role. He had no political training, no pressure group behind him; he relied solely on his own talents and was no Agar who could walk delicately. On the contrary, he marched in where less angelic men feared to tread. Had he been less gifted or had he ever had to make his own way in life, he might have been a more significant factor on the American scene. He would also have been a less attractive figure. There will always be

[10] *The Long Road Home*, p. 205.
[11] *The Long Road Home*, p. 206.
[12] *The Long Road Home*, p. 205.

admiration for the talented amateur, particularly when he tilts at windmills.

For the rest of his life Jimmy played a vigorous, but always peripheral, part in his country's political life. Almost always he was on the side of the angels, but all too often the angels were fighting a losing battle.

In the last quarter of his life he showed more percipience than ever before. In the spring of 1944, when victory was assured, he was asked by John J. McCloy, Assistant Secretary of War, for his views on the nature and purpose of the Allied occupation of Germany. He replied that it should be short and limited to ridding her of the Nazi party machine and helping her set herself on her own feet. The Germans must reform themselves. It was not long before Churchill was saying the same thing, but Jimmy's advice was rejected at the time as a policy that would induce chaos.

In the same year, in *Foreign Policy at Home* [13] he urged Britain and the United States to help underdeveloped countries become industrialized. Again he was ahead of his time. Most of them had not even been liberated.

In 1946, in *Unwritten Treaty*,[14] he called for an international agreement to ban all future political or psychological aggression through propaganda or subversive activity. In retrospect the plea seems idealistic to the point of silliness. Nonetheless, the same plea was put forward seventeen years later by the American delegation to the Geneva Disarmament Conference of 1962.

In 1947, amid the spate of books and pamphlets that were now coming from Jimmy's pen, he suggested, in *Germany, Bridge or Battleground*,[15] the formation of a European coal authority to settle once and for all the vexing problems of the Ruhr. He lived to see the establishment of the European Economic Community and the signing of the Treaty of Rome.

[13] New York: Harcourt, Brace & Co., 1944.
[14] New York: Harcourt, Brace & Co., 1946.
[15] New York: Harcourt, Brace & Co., 1947.

In affairs at home, Jimmy drifted steadily leftward in the postwar years. He was never remotely a man of the Left, but all his life he demanded fair play, and fair play for liberal ideas through the 1950s and up to the election of President John F. Kennedy was not a popular idea.

For this reason he financed, with Marshall Field, the establishment in Montgomery, Alabama, of a liberal newspaper, the *Southern Farmer*, which became a voice of sanity in a world of old-fashioned reaction. Within two years its circulation had risen from a hundred thousand to over a million.

In that same period he became an advisor and speechwriter for Sidney Hillman, president of the Amalgamated Clothing Workers of America and leader of the Congress of Industrial Organizations.

In the early 1950's when two of his closest friends, Owen Lattimore and Joseph Barnes came under vicious attack from Senator Joseph McCarthy, Jimmy publicly defended them at the risk of his own reputation.

In the early 1960's, Jimmy acted as one of the financial "angels" to the Institute for Policy Studies, in Washington, D.C., run by two severe critics of capitalism, Richard J. Barnet and Marcus G. Raskin.

To many of his social and business friends it must have seemed the grossest apostasy—that James P. Warburg, a Wall Street banker, should engage in such "leftist" activities.

But few people had any idea of the complex of emotionalism and business instinct that mingled in Jimmy. Obsessed by the evil of McCarthyism and dismayed by the witch-hunting mentality of those in power in the 1950s, he did not care in the least who his allies were in this fight against evil.

To the majority of his fellow Jews in America, his violent attack in 1959 on the United Jewish Appeal appeared in the same apostate light. He condemned the use of nontaxable charitable bequests for the purpose of buttressing the finances of the rival parties in the new State of Israel. In this instance he appeared to outdistance his cousins in his non-Zionist stance. But for the most part, he remained aloof from the affairs of Zion.

During these years he found his political idol in that most attractive of liberal-minded statesmen, Adlai E. Stevenson. By instinct Jimmy was a fighter for lost causes, and Stevenson was one of their leading standard-bearers. In the first of Stevenson's two unsuccessful presidential campaigns against Dwight D. Eisenhower in 1952 and 1956, Jimmy gave him his most active support, even helping to write Stevenson's speeches: "Stevenson's campaign from beginning to end set a new high in American politics. . . . Much as I had admired him, I had had only an inkling of the man's true greatness of heart and mind until it was unfolded during the grueling weeks of campaigning." [16]

Jimmy was certainly supporting a lost cause. After twenty years of Democratic rule the nation was eager to give a Republican candidate of the stature of General Eisenhower, Supreme Allied Commander of World War II, yet another victory.

Four years later Stevenson was again the Democratic presidential candidate, but this time Jimmy's support was, to put it mildly, lukewarm. Perhaps he felt that Stevenson's day was gone. His old idol fought against the heaviest odds. President Eisenhower's masterly inactivity during his first term had exactly suited the prevailing American mood. A second term was a foregone conclusion. Jimmy was growing older. Was he wearying of tilting at windmills?

In 1960 the Democratic party had once again a good chance. With a reluctant backward glance at his twice-defeated former idol, Jimmy cast his weight behind John F. Kennedy.

Nevertheless, his friendship with Stevenson remained outwardly unimpaired. In the closing years of Jimmy's life, Stevenson referred to him as "Citizen Extraordinary," and with perhaps a touch of cynicism, "In the great tradition of eighteenth century pamphleteers." [17]

16 *The Long Road Home*, p. 271.
17 *The Long Road Home*, p. 305.

Jimmy's critical pen had always been politically mightier than his sword of action.

Jimmy's attitude toward the Democratic nominees in the election of 1968—the last presidential campaign of his life—was characterized by his friend Joseph Barnes: "Jimmy had been a Stevenson man, then he was a [Eugene] McCarthy man. Finally he held his nose and voted for Humphrey."

He was by then largely disillusioned by politics. In any event illness had already precluded Jimmy's further active participation. Since 1961 he had been spending the winter in the new vacation house he and his third wife Joan had built in Florida and in the summer sought sanctuary in his house in Connecticut, which he had purchased in 1924. Less than an hour's drive from Manhattan, but deep in the wooded New England countryside, this long, low-slung home, with the adjacent barn he had converted into his library and study, gives an air of unobtrusive taste and comfort.

Jan Steen paintings hang on its walls, and the desk in Jimmy's workroom was his father's in his early days at Kuhn, Loeb.

The house and its furnishings contrast not only with the stuffy, overupholstered atmosphere in Frankfurt, from which his Oppenheim grandmother had come, but with his uncle Felix's highly ornate Fifth Avenue mansion. It resembles the home his cousin Eric has made for himself since the war on the banks of the Elbe.

John F. Kennedy was another of Jimmy's admirers: "I know of few Americans who have served the country so well in stimulating the discussion of foreign affairs," [18] he wrote to Jimmy, in 1961. It was a fine tribute to a man of remarkable achievements—as banker-economist, writer, and politician.

Yet it could also be said that James P. Warburg was in some senses a failure, a man who reached the foothills of fame but never climbed the dizzy heights. There was a basic contradiction between his conservative, capitalist banking training and his hard-won liberal

[18] *The Long Road Home*, p. 305.

and international convictions that led him into mistakes and mis-judgments.

But underlying the many apparent inconsistencies in his career was one stable factor. By his passionate prewar advocacy of the Allied cause long before the American public was willing to follow his lead, by his postwar opposition to the Cold War mentality of the majority of his fellow citizens and his belief in a regenerate Germany as a bastion of Western civilization, he showed himself a truly liberal man. There are too few of them alive today. It was fitting that in 1962 he should have been awarded the Gandhi peace prize.

❧ CHAPTER FIFTEEN

Siegmund and the City of London

FROM small beginnings four hundred years ago, the Warburg family rose to wealth and great influence in Germany. Through two marriages at the turn of the twentieth century they performed, far more rapidly, the same feat in the United States. In the first half of this century the Warburg pendulum swung steadily away from the Old toward the New World. Since the end of World War II it has swung back again, stopping this time in Britain as well as in Germany. Perhaps the most powerful Warburg alive today has his headquarters in the heart of the City of London. His name is Sir Siegmund Warburg.

Siegmund Warburg is of the stem of Jesse. His grandfather, also Siegmund, was the grandson of Moses Marcus, cofounder of M. M. Warburg & Sons, and the elder son of the matriarch Sara. With his younger brother Moritz, and always under the strict eye of their formidable mother, the first Siegmund advanced the fortunes of the family firm, and it was due largely to his initiative that Warburgs widened their activities in Germany from those of respected bill brokers into the more adventurous field of merchant banking.

Moritz was the last of the strictly orthodox Warburgs, unadventurous by nature, and an introvert by temperament.

Siegmund and the City of London

Siegmund was the first of the unorthodox Warburgs, sanguine by temperament, tolerant by nature, eager, like his grandson nearly a century later, for change.

On one occasion Moritz came to him in some consternation. One of the firm's employees had confessed that he would soon be the father of an illegitimate child, which of course meant he must be sacked at once.

Siegmund only said, "I hope the mother is a pretty girl."

Despite this cavalier moral attitude Siegmund faithfully attended religious services after deaths in the family, even if at least on one occasion he was clad in riding habit, and hastily departed as soon as the service was over to join the local hunt.

Siegmund the First died at 47. Between him and his grandson was interposed a man who, like his first cousin Aby, cared not a whit for banking. Aby chose art, and George chose agriculture.

"Farmer George" Warburg, Siegmund the Second's father, plowed the considerable fortune he had inherited from his own father into the development of a large farm near Stuttgart in the heart of Swabia. There he became widely respected as an agriculturist. He also found a most congenial neighbor in a certain Herr (later Baron) von Neurath, and the two families frequently exchanged courtesy visits. The young Siegmund was often in the family party which traveled in a horse-drawn barouche and Neurath took note of the boy's obvious intelligence. Neurath's career prospered, and he eventually became permanent under secretary at the German foreign office.

During the same period the young Siegmund was displaying considerable enterprise. Though his father had eschewed banking and all its works, still the world of finance was an obvious avenue to advancement for anyone with the name Warburg. Siegmund spent his apprenticeship first in Paris, then in New York with Kuhn, Loeb, where his uncles Paul and Felix were partners, and in the London headquarters of Rothschilds. (A young Rothschild was doing the same thing at Warburgs in Hamburg.)

In 1930, at the age of twenty-eight, he became a partner in his older cousin Max's Hamburg firm, and in the following year he started the first branch office of M. M. Warburg & Co. in Berlin.

During these years Siegmund was unofficially employed by his father's old friend Neurath as his eyes and ears in the world outside Germany, reporting in particular on the political and financial tendencies of the Western democracies, with which the Weimar Republic was allied. Siegmund continued to work for Neurath in this capacity even during the earliest days of the Hitler regime when the baron became, perhaps reluctantly, minister for foreign affairs.

But the burning of the Reichstag in February, 1933, resulted in savage anti-Jewish reaction, and the linking of Jews and Communists with the subversion of the Third Reich.

Siegmund confronted Neurath, telling him he must go straight to President Hindenburg and demand the dismissal of Hitler as chancellor. Neurath prevaricated, telling him that there was nothing in the laws of Germany that enabled the president to do anything of the sort.

Siegmund quoted the relevant article of the constitution of the Weimar Republic whereby the president could dismiss any chancellor who had violated the rights of the German people, and added—as Neurath well knew—that the then head of the German *Reichswehr* ("land and naval forces") was an anti-Nazi and would support any action Hindenburg might take.

It might have been an historical turning point, but Neurath refused to do what Siegmund asked.

He was not, he told his young protégé, himself a member of the Nazi party, and could not afford to jeopardize his already suspect position. Siegmund immediately understood the threat to himself behind Neurath's words. He telephoned his wife, then in Stockholm, and told her to meet him in London as soon as possible.

Siegmund's precipitate departure from Germany in 1933 caused a rift, never fully healed, between himself and his older cousin Max.

The latter accused him of betraying the cause of the Jews, and of Germany, by failing to stay and fight.

Siegmund countered by telling Max that it was he who was deceiving his fellow Jews by encouraging them, by his example, to remain in the face of their inevitable destruction. Siegmund prophesied at that time that war, with all it would entail for the German Jews, was going to come within two years. However, he did not take into account the spinelessness of the British and French governments, and 1935 dragged on into 1939.

Siegmund Warburg arrived in London with only £5,000 to his name. He was given a room in the offices of his cousin by marriage, Paul Kohn-Speyer, chairman of the firm of Brandeis Goldschmidt, and wrote to Neurath, thanking him for hinting to him to get out of Germany. With the assistance of funds provided from Holland, where the Merchants International Corporation acted for the Warburg banks in both Hamburg and Amsterdam, he founded his first British venture, the New Trading Company. But it was not a big operation, and in the ensuing years the City of London heard little or nothing of him. What use was there in building a future when a world war was so obviously imminent? As far as it was in his nature to do so, he lay low, financially speaking. During the war he served with British intelligence.

But in 1946 Siegmund Warburg founded the merchant-banking firm of S. G. Warburg & Co. Though the City of London was slow to realize it, a new power had risen in its midst. By 1956 Warburgs had taken over the much older bank of Seligman Brothers and Siegmund had become a member of the London Accepting Houses Committee.

His position on the Committee was Siegmund's first foothold in the Establishment, a guarantee and acknowledgment of his integrity and acceptability. A year later in 1957 he found himself in battle against practically the whole of it.

Meanwhile Siegmund's original £5,000 had grown. In the late

1950s the profits of Mercury Securities Limited (the holding company for Warburgs) were approaching £2 million a year.

The story of what became known as the "Aluminum War" of 1958–59, crucial to Siegmund's career, has been told many times. It involved the ailing British Aluminium Company, the chairman and managing director of which were two pillars of the Establishment: Viscount Portal had been the wartime chief of the British air staff, and Geoffrey Cunliffe was the son of a former chairman of the Bank of England.

Two American firms wanted to buy effective control of British Aluminium. Portal and Cunliffe had already made a private agreement with the Aluminum Corporation of America (ALCOA) that they would advise British Aluminium shareholders to accept ALCOA's bid. The other U.S. company in the bidding was the Reynolds Metals Company.

British Aluminium (and so ALCOA as well) was backed initially by Hambro's Bank and Lazards, the heart of the Establishment. Reynolds Metals Company officials sought the advice of Warburgs. Siegmund advised them to enter into partnership with the British firm of Tube Investments. Significantly, the head of Tube Investments, Sir Ivan Stedfort, was a totally self-made man with no Establishment connections.

As the bidding escalated, the Aluminum War made national headlines. At stake were not only profits but according to Portal and Cunliffe, British national prestige.

The Establishment rallied to the flag. A consortium of banking institutions, including Morgan, Grenfell, M. Samuel, Samuel Montagu, Guinness Mahon, and the British South Africa Company, combined with Hambros and Lazards to declare that a sale to Tube Investments would be against the national interest. Warburgs had one ally, Lionel Fraser, chairman of an older merchant bank, Helbert Wagg. He proved a trenchant supporter.[1]

[1] He proved an equally staunch friend to Fred Warburg when the firm of Thomas Tilling, of which he was chairman, took a controlling interest in the Heinemann Group of Companies. (See Chap. 20.)

In an interview with a London newspaper, Fraser expressed his scorn at the idea that shareholders should be advised to sell to an American company at sixty shillings a share when the price ruling on the stock exchange, and at which Tube Investments was prepared to buy, was eighty shillings.

"The whole thing," Fraser declared, "smacks of fear. It is unprogressive."

In the end not only the ordinary private investor but the big institutions, such as the insurance companies and the Church of England Commissioners, listened not to the consortium's jingoistic "Save British Aluminium for civilization" but to the more practical advice of the outsiders, Siegmund Warburg and Lionel Fraser. Within a short time Tube Investments had acquired 80 percent of British Aluminium shares—at a great profit to investors large and small. The battle was over. The outsiders had won. Portal and Cunliffe resigned their directorships.[2]

The result of the Aluminum War marked the end—as far as banking was concerned—of the "old-boy network." The Establishment had lost. The Establishment remained, but with new guidelines. Thenceforward prestige yielded to profitability, and the era of the bowler hat, stiff white collar, and striped trousers was at an end.

Reminiscing about his first great battle, Siegmund tends to look on it as a "make-or-break" affair. This is an exaggeration. Even if he had lost, he would have lived to fight another day. But his triumph in the winter of 1958–59 made him a power in the land.

Previously he had been, in the words of another banker, "unloved and unknown." He may still have been unloved afterward, but he was certainly not unknown.

Those he had defeated were bitter—Lord Kindersley, chairman of Lazards, declared, "I'll never shake that man by the hand again"—but their hatred was short-lived. Very soon another banker opponent was telling Siegmund that the City of London owed him

[2] A comprehensive account of the Aluminum War can be found in *The Merchant Bankers* by Joseph Wechsberg (New York, 1966) and *The Anatomy of Britain* by Anthony Sampsom (New York, 1972).

a debt of gratitude. He had made them sit up and think. Then, Sir Olaf Hambro, on his sickbed, sent a peace emissary to inquire whether Siegmund would come to see him. Soon he became *Sir* Siegmund. The Establishment had admitted him to their charmed circle, and on his terms.

During this period he made himself the master of the takeover bid. Siegmund advised the Canadian Lord Thomson in his successful bid for the Kemsley newspaper chain (whose chief ornament was the *Sunday Times*) and was at the elbow of Cecil King of the International Publishing Corporation in his fight with the same Lord Thomson for the control of Odhams Press. (Nonetheless, Sir Siegmund is today Lord Thomson's chief financial adviser.)

He has never yet been on the losing side in such an operation. In January, 1972, he was adviser for the defense in the attempted takeover of Trust Houses Forte by a big brewery company. Despite the fact that nearly half the board of THF was in favor of the takeover, it was defeated. It is again relevant that Lord Thomson, Sir Charles Forte, and to a lesser extent Cecil King had had to make their own ways in life. They were the new men, and Sir Siegmund was the new banker.

Later in 1972 S. G. Warburg was in the news again, this time as advisers to the Maxwell Joseph Group of Companies, Grand Metropolitan Hotels. Maxwell Joseph made a takeover bid for the old and highly reputable brewing concern, Watney, Combe, Reid. This battle highlighted a growing concern in business circles and among informed public opinion about the growth of giant corporations in control of manifold and often unrelated businesses. Were such multilateral and often—though not in the case of Grand Metropolitan Hotels—multinational monoliths really desirable? Many were coming to look on them as dangerous, all-devouring octopuses.

In January, 1973, *The Times of London* commented on a speech by Harold Wilson, leader of the Labor opposition, which voiced increasing anxiety about conglomerates:

Siegmund and the City of London

Many people are alarmed and frustrated by the extent to which they feel themselves to be pawns in other men's games. Their future, and that of their families, may be dependent not on their own endeavours—but on distant decisions over the allocation of industrial resources or on the subtle transactions of financiers.

The Aluminum War had been fought over an ailing concern, and at least the rival bidders were in the same business. Watneys, however, was far from sickly. The business was efficiently run, the profits respectable if not spectacular. The Maxwell Joseph interests had never previously been concerned with the brewing industry, except as a purchaser of beer for their hotels.

For a time, as figures and estimates of profits were bandied about and the battle spilled over from the financial to the news columns, it seemed that Sir Siegmund might be heading for his first defeat, and a defeat after a run of such brilliant successes could have been particularly damaging. In addition, the employees of Watneys were solidly behind their management, a psychological factor that came near to winning the day. But once again the Warburg magic worked. At the eleventh hour key institutions, including, it is believed, the "Pru" (the Prudential Assurance Company), threw their support to Maxwell Joseph. By a narrow margin the takeover bid went through, and Watneys was swallowed.

Siegmund Warburg is, and probably will always remain, an enigma. In private conversation he gives no glimpse of the hard, even ruthless, man of business that he undoubtedly is. (His employees work longer hours than practically anyone else in the City of London.)

His manner is soft-spoken, almost diffident. As you look at his wide brow you feel you are in the presence not of a banker but a thinker, a man who should eschew takeover bids, and instead, found institutes of learning like his cousin Aby. In fact, following in the footsteps not of Aby but of Fritz, he has endowed the Foundation of Graphological Science and Application attached to the University of Zurich. A classical scholar, he reads widely and is particularly fond of Thomas Mann's *Dr. Faustus*.

However, beneath a surface of Old World charm, Siegmund is an uncompromisingly modern man. More than any of his cousins he has adapted to the postwar world, and however much he may privately deplore its leveling tendencies, has made it work for him. He has no respect for tradition or the easy life. Classicist he may be, but he has scant use for confident young applicants who come to him with degrees from Oxford or Cambridge, who in his opinion have sacrificed real knowledge on the altar of a good degree. He has an acid test for these young men: If they should receive orders they believe to be ill-advised from an experienced superior, would they stand up and be counted? Only those who say yes are hired.

This most unorthodox of modern merchant bankers professes to believe that influence is far more important than power and likes to see himself in the role of a kind of family financial doctor dispensing critical wisdom, but always unobtrusively. His soft Swabian voice (his foreign accent is more marked than that of his Hamburg cousin Eric) lends credibility to this self-image. Personally, he has always shunned the limelight.

What good works he engages in, he does by stealth. He has been a large benefactor of the State of Israel, but no details have ever been disclosed. He gave financial support (totally unpublicized) to the new and brilliantly edited *Jewish Observer and Middle East Review* until its Jewish editor's endeavors to present the Arab as well as the Israeli point of view aroused the violent hostility of the Israeli government. On that occasion, it may be said, he backed down.

But he has always played the part of the man behind the scenes, the prompter rather than the leading actor. Moreover, his prompting has unfailingly been of value to those immediately concerned.

But are not influence and power in many ways identical? And do family doctors normally have such a shrewd eye for the main chance? It is not always those who seek the limelight who hold the real power.

Sir Siegmund's brilliant financial brain is powered by a steely resolution, as the British banking Establishment was forced to discover before they accepted him as one of their own.

It is arguable that this scholar-banker draws together the main strains of his variegated family in his own person and in his chosen field is the most powerful of them all. He can, as many will confirm, fascinate, almost mesmerize. He has made a great deal of money for himself, and a great deal more for others. He has enhanced the reputation of the City of London in a period when it may be the greatest of Britain's remaining assets. Whatever his personal aims, this Warburg has contributed much to his adopted country.

❧ CHAPTER SIXTEEN

Eric: The Rebuilder

ERIC WARBURG is the Warburg who returned after World War II to a defeated Germany to help rebuild what the Nazis had shattered. He could easily have remained in the United States where the prospects were brighter. He chose the more difficult course. His reward is the leading position that he and Warburgs' hold in Hamburg and all of West Germany today.

Max's only son, Eric was born in 1900. As a boy he witnessed the rapid expansion of the family firm under his father's leadership in the years before World War I. He was drafted for military service in 1918, but the Armistice was signed before he reached the front.

One of his sisters maintains that Eric was a soldier born. As a recruit, she recalls, he was surprised in the bath by a *Wehrmacht* officer inspecting the barracks. Eric sprang naked from the bath and saluted smartly. Many years later, after he had served with distinction in World War II as an American officer the aged Max told him, "A Jewish general we've never had, so better go back to Hamburg." A soldier born, perhaps; but a career officer? Never.

In his youth, like many young Warburgs before or since, he served his banking apprenticeship abroad, in his case in America with Kuhn, Loeb, and in London first with the nonferrous metal firm of Brandeis Goldschmidt and then, like his father, with N. M. Rothschilds in New Court. But America, so rich in Warburg cousins, was beckoning. In 1923 he went as a trainee to the International Acceptance Bank founded two years earlier by his uncle Paul.

Then, like others of his clan, he showed signs of wanting to break free of the constricting Warburg embrace. When Moritz Warburg summoned Max back to the rigors of banking in Hamburg, the latter had at first been loath to forsake the fleshpots of Paris and the *fin de siècle* elegance of London. A peremptory order from Max to return to New York was similarly resisted by his son.

Eric was in Oregon at the time. Sent there on business by his uncle Paul, he had fallen in love with this Rocky Mountain state and had broken away to take a job of his own at $100 a month—a very un-Warburgian salary.

At first Max acquiesced in his son's action and sent him $1,000 to buy a car. Then he changed his mind. Eric must return to banking. The first step: a return to his apprenticeship with uncle Paul in New York. Eric's reaction was to return the $1,000.

For a year father and son were deadlocked, then Max appealed to his favorite brother, Paul. Eric was persuaded to discuss the future with his uncle.

"My dear boy," Paul told him sternly, "there are those so unable to help themselves that they can only get out of a bath when they have pulled the plug. Others can't bring themselves even to pull the plug. So I am going to pull the plug for you. Come back to New York."

It was the end of Eric's "wild oats." [1]

Uncle Paul had settled Eric's career. For the foreseeable future he was destined, as his uncle before him, to be a transatlantic

---

[1] There is a sequel to this story. Over a decade later, in 1936, Eric was returning by boat from New York to Hamburg. Also on board was the young son of one of his father's friends. The boy could not make up his mind whether to emigrate. Eric told him the bath-plug story and concluded, "I have a father to look after in Germany. Your father and mother are dead. Pull the plug before it is too late." Sometime later Eric received a bouquet of roses tied with a plug and chain. The young man had taken his advice.

commuter, with one foot in the United States and the other in Germany.

From 1923 onward, Eric was a permanent resident of the United States, although he did not become a naturalized American citizen until 1938. He was made a partner in M. M. Warburg & Co. in the early 1930s and also held posts in the years between the two world wars with the International Acceptance Bank and other American financial concerns, including the American and Continental Corporation of New York City.

For a time he was chairman and executive vice-president of the Finnish-American Trading Corporation.

During these years, however, he remained, in the world's eyes, his father's son. He never overshadowed Max as Max had overshadowed Moritz. Though the judgment was unfair, he was widely regarded as his father's mouthpiece. He did not, at that time, attain a reputation and status comparable to that of his older cousin, Jimmy.

It was Jimmy the nephew, not Eric the son, who investigated the affairs of M. M. Warburg in 1931. It was another cousin—Siegmund—not Eric, who chided Max for refusing to face up to the Nazi menace before it was too late. To some extent at least Eric shared his father's view, "It can't happen to me." Yet his dual role and dual nationality at a critical moment provided a lifetime without which his father and his family might not have survived.

Eric was in Germany in 1938 when Max decided to sail to the United States, and he accompanied his father to New York.

Less than a year later Eric was back in Europe, in London. He joined the British Combat Intelligence Unit at the Air Ministry in London and was subsequently transferred to the newly formed Anglo-American Joint Combat Intelligence Unit. During this period, he discovered a previously unrealized ability as an interrogator.

After the United States entered the war in 1941, he became

chief interrogator, again stationed in London, for the U.S. Army Air Force. Later he held the same post in the field in North Africa and Sicily.

In June, 1944, holding the rank of colonel, he was the commanding officer of the Air Prisoners of War Interrogation Unit and took part in nearly every operation in Western Europe. His accomplishments were rewarded by the Croix de Guerre Étoile Vermeille from the French, the Order of the British Empire from the British, and the Legion of Merit from the Americans.

At the end of the war the British director of intelligence wrote to him praising his work in "laying the foundations of the strategic security of the United States and Great Britain." Discovering an exceptional competence he had not known he possessed and the opportunity to exercise it during the war years was a profound source of fulfillment for a man so long in his father's shadow. Yet there were times when Eric hated what he had to do. On one occasion he was confronted with a German officer who he suspected possessed important information. Under the rules of the Geneva Convention the prisoner was required to give only his name, rank, and serial number. However, the man was carrying thirty-five love letters from his mistress. Eric resorted to blackmail: "These letters will be returned to your wife through the International Red Cross," he told the officer.

The German, previously stubbornly silent, turned white as a sheet. "It is not enough," he cried, "that we will probably lose the war, and I will lose my job as a professional officer. Now you will destroy the last thing that I have—my family life."

Eric told him that for every worthwhile answer he gave he would get back one of these letters. All thirty-five were returned to him, "by which time we had learned all we wanted to know."

It was far from magnificent, but it was war, and in Eric's words: "War is ghastly in every detail."

Eric's wartime career was exciting and of great value to the cause he served, but it had its tragic overtones. Many of the young flyers he had to interrogate were, he knew, untainted by Nazism. They were patriotic young Germans fighting for the fatherland, and however distorted the image had become, it was Eric's fatherland too.

But about one man he had no qualms. Eric was the first man to interrogate Field Marshal Hermann Göring, after his capture in 1945.

Göring was a willing talker. First he summarized his full titles—*Reichsminister* for air, supreme commander of the German Air Force, prime minister of Prussia, president of the state council, president of the Reichstag, Reichsmaster of forestry and game, president of the Scientific Research Council. The titles summarized his conception of himself—airman, statesman, politician, scientist, a superman of the Third Reich.

Yet under his interrogator's skillful guidance this self-image vanished. The *Reichsmarschall* launched into what developed into an *apologia pro vita sua*.

In Eric's view, before his arrest Göring had been living partly in a dream world. The dream world showed in Göring's account of the consequences of the telegram he sent to Hitler on April 23, 1945, announcing that he was taking full control of the Reich. He called it the most moving moment of his life when he was hailed by those elements of the S.S. which supported him as "Commander-in-Chief."

A few days later the "commander-in-chief" was captured by the Americans, and the dream had vanished, to be replaced, under interrogation, by a shrewd but futile attempt to shift the blame. He suggested that though he might have made errors Hitler must take all the blame for such matters as the saturation bombing of unde-fended British cities (even though Göring was head of the *Luftwaffe*).

Göring knew Hitler had become an archfiend for both the Americans and the British and so he represented himself, in con-trast, as rather a good fellow. In fact, he said, he was a good

European. His only real enemy had been the Soviet Union. He had never had anything to do with the Nazi party and had always put the welfare of the state first.

In his assessment of Göring's character Eric had an advantage lacking to the judges of the Nuremberg Trials a year later. When confronted only a few days after his capture by this calm and apparently dispassionate observer, Göring must have hoped that he might be able to save his skin and was more willing to talk. Eric's final verdict was that the once daring fighter ace had turned soft after years of luxurious living.

One of Göring's statements to Eric, the latter will always remember: "I have never signed a man's death warrant, or sent anyone to a concentration camp, never, never, never, unless of course it was a question of expediency." To hear these words from a man who had been indirectly responsible for the persecution and murder of millions of his co-religionists must have been a very traumatic experience.

After his interrogation of Göring, Eric's wartime career drew to a close. What his postwar career would be seemed clear. He would return to the United States—after all, he was an American citizen, and his father, always to him the great Max—was still alive and concerning himself with the business of E. M. Warburg which Eric had founded in the thirties. Two of his sisters were in America, and he was assured of the affection of his cousins, the children of Felix and Paul.

Besides, the Warburg name had been obliterated in Germany. Why should Eric concern himself with the affairs of a bank now trading under the name of Brinckmann, Wirtz? Or indeed with a nation that had robbed his family of much of their fortune and proclaimed them and their fellow Jews traitors and degenerates?

Then he received a summons from John McCloy, the American member of the joint Allied heads of military government for all Germany. Would he, McCloy asked, leave the United States and return to Hamburg, resume his previous career there, and help to rebuild the shattered fabric of this much bombed and least Nazi of all German cities, where his father had been so prominent a citizen?

It is not hard to understand the reasoning behind McCloy's suggestion. Of all the German refugees at large in America and Britain, Jew or Aryan, Eric was for McCloy and many others the best qualified to act as a bridge-builder between the recent foes. His American references were impeccable. Given the eclipse of the Nazis, so were his German ones. The family name was a household word in Hamburg, and in World War I his father had been, without qualification, a patriotic citizen. His family's loyalty had been reaffirmed by their departure only at the eleventh hour from Hitler's Germany.

In the eyes of leading Allied soldiers and statesmen, bridge-building was urgently necessary. The Potsdam Conference had given a clear indication of the cold war to come. Winston Churchill in his "Iron Curtain" speech at Fulton, Missouri, had already articulated the danger.

McCloy's request posed an agonizing choice for Eric. On the one hand, west of the Atlantic was security and prosperity. On the other, at the mouth of the Elbe lay opportunity, perhaps, but the likelihood of hostility and great unhappiness as well. How many of those who had cold-shouldered him or his father in the prewar Nazi days would still regard him as a traitor to Germany? How genuine, even in Hamburg, was the eclipse of the Third Reich?

Eric's positive response to the request showed great courage, but he was also careful to provide a measure of insurance. He would return to Hamburg as a private citizen, but he would sever none of his American links.

For the next four years he was once again a transatlantic commuter. It was not until 1950 that he made the bank in Ferdinand-strasse and the house in Kösterberg more than *pieds-à-terre*.

How did he come to make this decision?

Eric's reaction to the years of horror the Jews of Germany had lived through was largely atypical. In a recent book, *The American*

Jews,[2] James Yaffe wrote that the basic Jewish attitude is that all Germans are Nazis and always will be Nazis, that the slightest sign of neo-Nazi sentiment in Germany is greeted with shrill horror, and that this feeling is so strong that it persists even among those who struggle to overcome it.

Eric's youngest sister, Gisela, who married Judge Wyzanski of Boston, took her eight-year-old son on a European tour seven years after the war's end, ending up at Kösterberg.

There were woods to be explored, a swimming pool to enjoy, trees to be climbed. There were young Germans of his age to make friends with. After their return to their Boston home, his mother took him to see a German Jewish refugee friend.

"What," asked the friend, "did you enjoy most in Europe?"

"I liked Germany best."

Deeply shocked, the friend later asked Gisela, "How *could* you let your son say that?"

When she told her son of this comment, Gisela received the simple reply: "Mother, the boys I played with know as little of Hitler as I do."

Gisela saw the force of her son's remark. But did she *feel* it? Even today she admits that though she feels unhappy if the United States or Israel behaves foolishly or immorally, in the case of Germany it is only what she expects. Her brother Eric, she adds, reacts quite differently. When Germany doesn't behave well, he is the first to proffer excuses.

Eric Warburg returned to Germany because he looked on the Nazi nightmare as an aberration outside the mainstream of German history. All his life, he has deeply admired Germany's cultural heritage.

Initially he had to face the sycophancy accorded him as a "conquering hero" by those who had previously reviled him and his

[2] New York: Random House, 1968, p. 57.

fellow Jews, and the uncertainty of other decent citizens as to whose side he was really on.

Was he a Trojan horse? Or a very forgiving man?

The final verdict is shown by his current position, and like his father before him, as Hamburg's leading banker.

During the years immediately after the war, whether as a member of the American armed forces, or later as a private citizen, Eric had ample opportunity to watch the workings of the Allied military government in the four occupied zones of Germany.

The British, in Eric's view, excelled. They knew what they were doing and had civil servants trained in many lands for many years. When they got out they left behind at least a measure of goodwill. Next best were the Americans, who had good intentions but little knowledge of how to put them into effect. Next, the French—who had no policy save to milk the country even when there was no milk left. Lastly, the Russians—and even more so, their handmaidens, the Poles, who exceeded even the French in their treatment of German victims.

The estate at Kösterberg to which Eric returned, first as an uncertain commuter, later as a confident resident, was superficially much as it had been when he had left it in 1938.

The antiaircraft installation that had been set up on the grounds had somehow escaped the attentions of Allied bombers, and Kösterberg was unscarred. Before the war Max and Fritz had given shelter in one of the three main houses to Jews awaiting their chance to emigrate. In 1945 Kösterberg again became a refugee center, limited mainly to convalescents from the concentration camps and from the Jewish Hospital in Hamburg. Also admitted were Jewish boys and girls—Polish as well as German—who were willing to be trained for work with the Zionist fighters of the Haganah in Israel.

Would Uncle Felix have approved?

In 1946 Eric brought his bride Dorothea to Kösterberg, and made her chatelaine of the smallest of the three houses. Herself a

Jewish refugee from Nazi persecution in Vienna, she had been living in Canada since before the war.

Initially strongly opposed to Eric's final return to Hamburg in 1950, the former Dorothea Thorsch had a far more difficult task than her husband in adapting herself to a return to Europe. She was forced to, and did in the end, successfully put down new roots where Eric had only to resuscitate old ones. But she could never bring herself to explicitly share her husband's belief in the regeneration of Germany.

Eric was more lenient in accepting the protestations of old friends and neighbors who had gone along with the Nazi regime that they had never known what was really happening, that the discovery of the concentration camps had horrified them as much as it did the soldiers who unearthed them. Dorothea Warburg kept her own counsel—but her two eldest children are American citizens.

The "Dutch House," as Eric's present residence is called, is an architectural gem in contrast with the solid Victorian structures that comprise the rest of the Kösterberg complex. Built in 1796, its name gives its provenance. Standing on the crown of the hill that rises steeply from the Elbe, its wooden frame and wide balconies give a feeling of space and light.

Here on Friday evenings Eric, his son, and two daughters gather in preparation for a weekend's sailing in the Baltic or Skaggerak—a passion he inherited from his father. Here open house is kept for friends of the Warburgs from many nations. The Dutch House does not possess the grandeur of Uncle Felix's Fifth Avenue mansion or White Plains estate. In its atmosphere of informal comfort it resembles Jimmy's house in Connecticut, far more closely. Both houses express their owners' lack of ostentation, the *gemütlich* quality that is a feature of the Warburg ambience.

A hundred yards down the hill stands "Elsa Brandström's House." Although Elsa Brandström is not related to the Warburg family she has played an important part in their lives, particularly in the lives of Fritz and Anna Warburg, who became her closest friends. During World War I, she accompanied her father to Petrograd (now Leningrad), where he was serving as the Swedish Ambassador. She quickly became aware of the cruelty and medical inefficiency that was common practice. Once, witnessing a flogging of German prisoners of war by cossack soldiers, she turned on a Russian officer, saying, "This is not war, it is swinery."

She took and passed the Russian Red Cross examinations, and for the next two years played the part of a second Florence Nightingale. Her drive, her ruthless cutting of red tape, her skills and humanity saved many thousands of lives.

Subsequently, she married a German Socialist. Her work, often in collaboration with Anna Warburg, brought her such renown that Hitler offered her the post of head of the German Red Cross. Her reply was brief and contemptuous: "Never." Shortly afterward, she was forced into exile.

The house Eric named for her is now a holiday home where young mothers can bring their children, hand them over to a trained staff, and enjoy themselves, free of the cares of domesticity. In the big room with the great bow-fronted window where Moritz and Charlotte once sat, these mothers can watch television—or the shipping on the Elbe.

The third Kösterberg house is a recreation center for young social workers from all over the world, and, like Elsa Brandström's house, has been donated by Eric.

Today, Eric is the patriarch of the present-day Warburgs, just as his cousin Carola Rothschild is the matriarch.

He is head of the family bank in Hamburg. He and his cousin Siegmund own a substantial part of the Effektenbank Warburg A.G. in Frankfort. Eric is a key figure in the Warburg story, for he links an older and a younger generation.

❧ CHAPTER SEVENTEEN

The Younger Generation

OF THE four young men who once marched with their father Felix five abreast down Fifth Avenue only one survives. Frederick died in 1973, Gerald predeceased him in 1971, Paul died in 1965. Only Edward remains. Like their cousin Jimmy all four were educated at the Middlesex School in Massachusetts, and all went to Harvard. All considered themselves preeminently Americans.

Frederick (Freddy), the eldest, was a year older than Jimmy. He was confirmed by Judah Magnes, but from then on his education followed Gentile lines.

Middlesex is first of all a boarding school (in itself an innovation for the Warburg family) and run on Unitarian lines. It is designed for the children of the rich, a forcing house for the Ivy League universities, especially Harvard. Freddy thrived in this atmosphere—he had an extraordinary ability to get on with everyone—and was for many years president of the Middlesex Alumni Association. In later life he was to become president of the Harvard Alumni Association as well.

His educational achievements at Harvard were unspectacular, but his three years on the banks of the Charles River set the pattern of his life. His Ivy oration to the Class of 1919, with its mixture of sentiment and banter, its gently snide references to the rival Yale, is very college-boy American.

Freddy aspired to belong to a different social caste than that described by Stephen Birmingham in *Our Crowd*. Its members would in due course proceed, often through family connections, to positions of authority on Wall Street and in the big American corporations, usually the exclusive terrain of Wasps. Freddy did likewise. The family connections were, of course, Jewish, but as perhaps the most assimilated of all his family, Freddy was well equipped to shrug off anti-Semitic attitudes and to be accepted in Ivy League circles.

It was inevitable that as the eldest grandson of Jacob Schiff, banking should claim him. After a brief spell in the army at the end of World War I followed by an apprenticeship with his uncle Max at M. M. Warburg in Hamburg, he duly entered Kuhn, Loeb in 1925. Apart from a six-year spell with the closely allied firm of Lehman Brothers and a period in the army during World War II, when he became chief of athletics and recreation in Special Services, he spent all his working life in the firm his maternal grandfather had made famous, eventually becoming its senior partner. As a banker he proved effective, hard-working if conservative, outwardly far more dedicated to the world of finance than his father had ever been. But his heart lay elsewhere.

When Frederick was at Harvard one of the consuming interests of many of his fellow undergraduates was sports.

In his Harvard Class of 1919 address, Freddy remarked: "We entered college when it was at its best from an undergraduate point of view—athletics on the crest, studies in the dumps!"

Lawn tennis was his forte as a young man, and it was he who brought the stars of Wimbledon and Forest Hills to the tennis courts at his father's estate in White Plains. History does not record how many games he won from them.

Later he became very interested in horses. His younger brother Edward gives him full credit for being a successful banker but adds, "He would have much preferred being editor of *Sports* magazine." The stud he founded at Williamsburg, Virginia, is one of his legacies. It had its foundations in a 1936 tour of the Virginia countryside in which Freddy's mentor and guide, the story goes, was the future Duchess of Windsor. He fell in love (with the countryside) and two years later purchased an estate and built a house. From that moment on, Middleburg, Virginia, became his home, and his Riverview Terrace apartment in New York was reduced to an appendage. Presiding over his Virginia estate Freddy dispensed the somewhat acid wit for which he became famous. Freddy was the first sporting American Warburg.

In his many charitable activities, however, he was faithful to family tradition, above all to the tradition of his father. His benefactions were often slanted toward youth.

He was a trustee of Smith College and closely associated with the Boy Scout movement. He worked for the National Recreation Association and was for a time treasurer of the New York Herald Tribune Fresh Air Fund. He succeeded Felix as a trustee of the American Museum of Natural History and funded the Felix M. Warburg Memorial Hall, opened there in 1951.

The hall was a tribute to the role his father had played in establishing Bear Mountain State Park in New York as a place where children could see animals and plants in their natural habitat.

He was, like all his brothers and his sister, devoted to his father's memory, but he did not interest himself in Felix's main preoccupations, the affairs of world Jewry and the international Zionist controversy. He summed up his attitude with the succinctness that was second nature to him: He felt "nearer to Bunker Hill than to Megiddo."

The musical strain in the family had been first evidenced in the early nineteenth century by Pius, the Altona Warburg, and by an unidentified Warburg given a letter of recommendation by Mendelssohn to the conductor of the Hamburg Orchestra at about the same time. It came to its fullest fruition in the person of Gerald

Warburg, who, many think, if he had had to earn his living, might have become a cellist of the very first rank. In any event his inherited wealth enabled him to do much for music. His connection was lifelong and of great distinction. It began almost as soon as he could stand upright, when he started to pump the pedals of his father's electric Pianola. It continued under the auspices of his aunt Nina, who arranged for him to have lessons on the half-sized cello owned by her younger brother. It was crystallized when Nina took him, at the age of eight, to a violin recital by Fritz Kreisler.

That evening determined Gerald's career. Founder and member of the well-known Stradivarius Quartet, which played throughout the United States and in many European countries, he had made his debut as a cello soloist in Vienna at the age of twenty-three. In the same year he performed with the New York Philharmonic Orchestra.

His subsequent crowded career included a great deal of work outside the concert hall. He was a prime mover in the foundation of the Violoncello Society, vice-president of the New York City Center, and gave many lectures on music on radio and television, including a series on the life and works of Beethoven. He commissioned a work, "Sacred Services" by Ernest Bloch, which is widely used as a musical setting in Jewish synagogues. He made a much-sought-after recording of Delius's *Double Concerto* for violin and cello with the London Royal Philharmonic Society. He was for several years conductor of the Brooklyn Symphony Orchestra.

Comparatively late in his life Gerald acquired what became his most treasured possession, the famous "Duport" Stradivarius cello.

Fact and legend mingle in the story of this remarkable instrument. Cremona, in northern Italy, was the home of Stradivarius, the greatest of all violin and violoncello makers, and it was there in 1711 that Stradivarius built the instrument that two centuries later came into Gerald's possession.

Jean-Louis Duport, its first owner, was a very great cellist. It is reasonably certain that Duport played this instrument before the king of Prussia (a cellist himself), and that in 1796 he gave the first performance of Beethoven's two cello sonatas before the same patron, with Beethoven himself at the piano. It is more than possible that the cello subsequently passed into the possession of the Empress Marie-Louise of Austria, at whose court Duport had also played. It is absolutely certain that Marie-Louise became the second wife of the Emperor Napoleon I of France.

Thereafter, however, legend takes over. There is a slight gash across the base of the instrument. Did Napoleon, holding the cello between his thighs and unable to produce any reasonable noise out of it, slash at it with his spur as an expression of his displeasure? Such was the story put out by Gerald's publicity agents. Fortunately for all those who like a touch of romance in history, it cannot be *dis*proved.

When the author visited Gerald Warburg in his 79th Street apartment a year before his death he took him into the special room where the Stradivarius was kept and after some pressure had been brought to bear, played this superbly toned instrument for five minutes.

Gerald Warburg was a modest, courteous man, reluctant to talk about himself or his career and preferring to discuss the father he so obviously adored. One of his favorite anecdotes described how Felix always stoutly protested his love of classical music and contempt for popular musical comedy, only to be heard whistling the latest Jerome Kern or George Gershwin song Gerald had just played on the piano.

In some ways Gerald was another Warburg exception, with little interest in banking, politics, or the Zionist controversy, yet he possessed an intense family loyalty.

When he came of age, his father prophesied in a birthday letter to him: "What the next years will bring is in your hands. . . . You are the most gifted of our sons, as far as natural gifts are concerned, and we hope that your life will be rich in joy for you and joy that you give to others."

He was not far wrong. What came into Gerald's hands was the cello, and he gave great joy to others, not only from the concert platform, but in his personal life.

The joy that he gave to others. The phrase is equally applicable to Gerald's younger brother Paul (affectionately known to hundreds of friends as "Piggy" because of his roly-poly figure and voracious appetite), from whom in other ways he differed so markedly. It represented Piggy's most important contribution to life. By Warburg standards he could be ranked as a failure—he climbed no heights, he plumbed no depths. He didn't want to. With one possible exception late in his life, he took very little seriously.

He rubbed shoulders with the great and rendered them some service, but it was social service, and not in the sense that the do-gooders of the world use the word.

He acted, for example, as a coordinator for Robert D. Murphy, the political adviser to General Eisenhower in the World War II North African campaign, and as a special assistant at the American embassy in Paris when it was reopened in 1944. Crossing the Channel he filled a similar role in the London embassy. His mother Frieda sums up perfectly his life in those immediate postwar years:

He spent a wonderful year in London, living with Ambassador Harriman first at Claridge's Hotel while the official residence was being prepared and then in the Residence. He became well acquainted with all the members of the Royal Family and with the leaders of the Socialist Government then in power. When Mr. Harriman resigned to become Secretary of Commerce, Paul stayed on for three years as special assistant to the new Ambassador, Lewis Douglas. Those were happy years for Paul, working with Mr. Douglas and his charming wife Peg, and their daughter Sharman.

Together they weathered the Berlin crisis, the Socialist Government, and the social life of London, as Paul likes to say, and all returned reluctantly to the United States in December 1950.

Paul's life was in general busy, and rather aimless. Like his cousin Jimmy he worked for a while for the Baltimore & Ohio Railroad and then in the International Acceptance Bank. After the latter had been merged with the Bank of Manhattan he became vice-president with the special task of attracting the accounts of high-salaried members of the film industry.

His mother wrote: "Paul made yearly trips to California for a time, in connection with this work, and became friendly with many stars, including Dolores del Rio, Miriam Hopkins and Eddie Cantor, as well as such sports stars as Babe Ruth."

Later Paul was to hold another vice-presidency—of the English-Speaking Union. He was well equipped to be *vice*-president of many organizations, but to be the actual head, the top man, that was another matter. It is doubtful that Paul ever aspired to such a position.

Throughout his life Paul, like all the American Warburgs, gave generously in money—if more sparingly in time—to many charities, Jewish and otherwise. But there was one particular charitable project which fully engaged his heart and his energies.

Started in the early 1950s, "Project Hope" involved the manning and equipping of a teaching hospital on a large ocean liner. Staffed entirely by volunteer, unpaid doctors it traveled around the world, stopping wherever it was invited (and nowhere else). From West Africa to South America the staff of Project Hope cooperated with the local doctors, and on its departure left a teaching team behind. The international flavor of this project, which reached its tenth anniversary before Paul died, was one of its chief appeals, for if his father Felix was the most flamboyant and his cousin Jimmy the most protean, Paul was certainly the most cosmopolitan of all the Warburgs.

"Impish, warm, generous, incorrigible" (the words are those of a man who knew him intimately), he regarded the whole Western world as his oyster, and delighted in its flavor. Edward, his younger brother, has described him as "a hopeless student, he enjoyed life too much!" In conversations with many people about the subjects of this book, there has been an almost invariable refrain, "And then of course there was Piggy." It is not a bad epitaph.

As a small boy Edward Warburg, the youngest of Felix's children, was nicknamed by his German nurse "Matz" (sparrow). His eldest brother promptly called him "Peep-Matz," a sparrow that peeped. When his mother objected, Freddy economized and re-christened him "Peepers." This name stuck.

When, like his brothers before him, he went to Middlesex School, one of his first encounters ran as follows:

An older boy: "Aren't you a wop?"

Edward [totally ignorant of what his questioner meant, but anxious to please]: "Well, I suppose so."

Older boy: "No, I mean, aren't you a Warburg?"

Edward: "Yes."

Older boy: "Well, they were all known as wops here."

To be called "Peepers" at home and "wop" at school, and later to be excluded from all the Harvard clubs because he was a Jew, might have proved a severe handicap to a sensitive boy—and there are no insensitive Warburgs. If it did, he certainly shrugged it off, just as, when a small boy, he shrugged off Jacob Schiff's stifling orthodoxy. (One Sabbath day Eddie picked a rose to present to his grandfather. Schiff responded: "You have killed something on the Sabbath.")

From Middlesex Eddie went to Harvard and began his artistic education. One of the proctors for the freshmen was James Rorrimer, later director of the Metropolitan Museum of Art. It was he who pointed out to Eddie the beauties of a Rembrandt etching which Felix had given him.

"It was this," Eddie wrote, "plus the exposure at the Fogg Museum to highly prized works which were equally meaningless to me, which plunged me into a long search for that subtle and elusive quality that made a work of art meaningful."

It was a search that led him to many places—he took time off from Harvard to travel to Britain to see a famous exhibition of Italian art at Burlington House—furnished much excitement, and produced at least two famous purchases.

On a visit to Germany in the early 1930s he bought Picasso's *Blue Boy* for a mere $7,000. At the customs shed at New York's Pier 90 he declared it at $4,000. A kindly customs official insisted that he reduce it to $2,000. Arrived at 1109 Fifth Avenue, it met with a violently hostile reception—his mother and father thought it obscene and banished it to the fifth floor.

Late in the 1930s, Eddie bought his friend Paul Klee's *Departure of the Ships* for $800. After World War II he sold it for $62,000. Few of his banker relatives, past or present, could boast of transactions yielding such a high profit.

James Rorrimer had set Eddie on the artistic road; it was Lincoln Kirstein, today director of the New York City Ballet, who became probably the most important influence on him—as well as a lifelong friend.

When Eddie first met him at Harvard, Kirstein had already founded with his friend John Walker an undergraduate magazine called *The Hound and Horn*, with the typical youthful ambition of publishing works by young writers and poets throughout the world. Eddie joined the editorial staff.

The three of them rented two rooms in Cambridge, where in addition to the magazine they founded the Harvard Society of Contemporary Art. It was to organize the first showings of works by Picasso, Matisse, Braque, and Derain ever to take place in those harbingers of European culture, the states of New England. They meant this society to be a deliberate challenge to the well-established, and to them, far too staid Fogg Museum, which nonetheless had been a strong influence on Eddie's artistic education. He was becoming a champion of the avant-garde, and chosen by his classmates as class orator, delivered a violent attack on Harvard's art department, which his father had helped found.

From art and literature he moved to music, and above all, to ballet. Here again Lincoln Kirstein led the way. In the 1920s, when all of Europe worshiped the Russian ballet under Diaghilev and later under de Basil, America had no national ballet at all. If Americans wanted to see *Swan Lake* or an exciting modern ballet like *Petrouchka* or *Le Tricorne* they must wait for a touring company to cross the Atlantic.

Then, one spring day in the early 1930s, Kirstein telegraphed from New York to Eddie at White Plains. He had just returned from Paris where he had met the choreographer George Balanchine. He had persuaded him to visit New York to explore the possibility of starting a ballet school that would lay the foundations of a native American ballet company. All that was needed to clinch the deal was the guarantee of round-trip fares from Paris to New York for Balanchine and his business associate M. Dimitriev. Kirstein would pay for one if Eddie would pay for the other. Though he privately considered the idea to be Kirstein's "latest madness," Eddie agreed.

"Little," he wrote later in his unpublished memoirs, "did I know at the time just what I was letting myself in for."

In a very short time Lincoln Kirstein had achieved an enormous amount. First he enlisted the support and enthusiasm of the director of the Wadsworth Atheneum in Hartford, Connecticut, who offered his new theater and auditorium as the focus for the projected ballet school. The news spread, and soon a long queue of aspiring ballerinas was asking to join.

Kirstein also spread the news that Balanchine was on his way. When he arrived in New York, a shy, gentle, precise little man, he brought with him a great bear of a Russian businessman named Dimitriev, with, to quote Eddie, "ice water in his veins and a constant smile which revealed voracious clenched teeth."

Very soon Balanchine and Dimitriev decided that if they were to start a ballet school—which if plenty of money was provided, they were graciously prepared to do—it should not be in provincial Hartford but in the glamorous metropolis of New York.

Lawyers were summoned, contracts were drawn up, and Eddie and Kirstein pledged their resources to give or raise the money needed. A studio was opened on Madison Avenue at Fifty-ninth Street, a grand enough address. The would-be ballerinas arrived, accompanied by what Eddie called "their God-awful mothers." The enrollment grew rapidly, and so did the outlay of capital and the increases in Balanchine's and Dimitriev's salaries. Careless of money, Balanchine and Kirstein planned the wildest extravagances while Dimitriev "lured us deeper into their commitments of this venture."

Yet Eddie could not resist the lure of watching Balanchine constructing his ballets, making music come to life through the gestures and movements of the dancers. In the end, his fascination cost him a great deal of money.

Four ballets were soon ready for performance, but where to perform them? No theatrical management was likely to risk an untried ballet company, but unless active and paid employment could be provided for the embryo dancers they would just melt away.

Eddie provided the solution. He persuaded his parents to let him stage an impromptu "gala performance" in celebration of his birthday on the grounds of their country house at White Plains.

Two hundred guests were invited, primitive spotlights were erected, and a piano hidden in the bushes. When all was ready for the first performance ever of Balanchine's now famous *Serenade*, with music by Tchaikovsky, the lights up, the dancers poised, a violent thunderstorm drenched dancers and audience alike.

Undismayed, the intrepid impresarios tried again the next night, this time in fine weather and to great applause. "It opened the way," Eddie said, "to the tortuous climb which took many years, until Balanchine and Lincoln [Kirstein], with the school, developed many generations of dancers, some of whom are now part of the glory of Lincoln Center."

The climb was indeed tortuous, and for Eddie, to put it mildly, unrewarding financially. Quite soon Balanchine had prepared a whole repertoire of ballets, but what was still needed, even after the success at White Plains, were performing outlets, not to mention costumes and scenery. Somehow—out of Eddie's pocket?—the latter two were provided, and performances were given in Hartford, and a few in New York, but audiences were scattered sparsely through the theater, and ballet critics who might have stimulated interest were at that time nonexistent in America. Eddie and his colleagues decided they should plan a transcontinental tour. For this a manager was needed. They picked on one R. Mirovich, then handling a tour by Chaliapin and the Don Cossack choir. He agreed to take them on an eleven-week tour.

The choice proved disastrous. They got as far as Scranton, Pennsylvania, about two hundred miles from New York, only to find after an evening's performance that Mirovich had pocketed all the money from the box office, declared himself insane, and disappeared. With their tails between their legs, with the dancers, the stagehands, and the musicians clamoring for their wages, Kirstein and company slunk back to New York. Yet such was the enthusiasm and genius of Balanchine and Kirstein, and the love of the arts displayed by Eddie, for years the venture's chief financial backer, that it survived. "Today," he could write with justice, "the New York City Ballet can hold its own with any Company in the world."

A devoted son, Eddie continued after Felix's death many of his father's philanthropic activities. In particular he succeeded him as chairman of the Joint Distribution Committee, holding the post for twenty-five years, and served for three years as national chairman of the United Jewish Appeal.

But he is of the younger generation. Like his brothers he did not become involved in the passions aroused by Zionist politics, already dying down with the establishment of Israel as an independent state.

Eddie has paid more than thirty visits to Israel, valuing them as "a wonderful way to recharge my batteries and to rediscover the basic verities of human dedication." But his tone is a far cry from his father's emotional attitude forty years earlier—if equally far from Jimmy's indifference.

As soon as the United States entered World War II Eddie volunteered for the army. But he was to remain a civilian in uniform rather than a warrior. Assigned to the provost marshall section at the headquarters of the Eastern (Atlantic Coast) Defense Command, he was charged with drafting a field order about the handling of the civilian population in the event of attack, sabotage, or other disaster. His colonel's comment: "This isn't a field order, it's a piece of literature." The incident is typical of Eddie's versatility as well as his lack of martial qualities.

As an officer trained in civilian affairs and military government in London, he landed on the Normandy beaches on D-Day plus one, charged with the care of refugees.

In Paris six weeks later, he visited the derelict offices of the Joint Distribution Committee. Its sole guardian was one very deaf old gentleman who told him that the Jews of Paris were practically destitute. That same night Jewish soup kitchens, organized by Eddie, appeared on the streets. The next morning he sent to the JDC headquarters in London, by the hand of Lord Rothschild, a message authorizing the immediate raising in New York of $65,000 for refugee relief. Read out to a mass meeting, his message resulted in the subscription of almost double that amount.

Just before the final German collapse at the beginning of May, 1945, Major Eddie Warburg found himself a member of the Supreme Headquarters Allied Expeditionary Force (SHAEF) mission to Belgium, where his immediate superior was an American colonel. (Eddie later commented: "We were glad that the mission was dissolved when it was, because his left bosom at that time no longer had room for further self-recommended decorations. War was not hell for [the] Colonel.")

One day this officer summoned Eddie to his office under conditions of absolute secrecy, and to quote Edmund Lear, "solemnly addressed him thus:"

"Warburg, the most important mission that has ever faced this headquarters is now coming up."

Eddie, it transpired, was to be entrusted with it. "I thanked the colonel and asked whether I might know what this mission consisted of."

The reply was that Eddie would be informed in due course. Meanwhile, only three people knew its purpose.

Eddie knew better. "I had been in the army long enough to know that there is never anything that only the general and a couple of colonels know about, because inevitably there is the sergeant who wrote it down."

He sought out the sergeant, who replied succinctly, "The king."

The "king" the sergeant was referring to was Leopold of Belgium who had remained in his country throughout the Nazi occupation, collaborating with his German masters. On the eve of the German collapse, Leopold had been taken to Germany, to an unknown location. When his brother and the Belgian government in exile returned from Britain, it was thought to be necessary to find Leopold. For one thing, though Eddie was not aware of it at the time, Leopold was not only the ruler of the Belgian Congo, Belgium's largest and most important colony, but its owner. The Americans received most of their uranium supplies from the Congo and wanted to insure that their source would not dry up in the war's aftermath.

Leopold had to be found, conciliated, cajoled. He was believed to be somewhere in the Tyrolean Alps.

From the SHAEF mission in Belgium there issued a top-secret document detailing a plan called "Operation Lion," which ran to fifteen instructions plus two appendices. The plan covered every eventuality and ensured that at least a hundred people would shortly be aware of its "top-secret" contents. Many more were to become aware that something odd was happening, as the search party set forth.

The group assembled at 5:30 A.M. at the royal palace in Brussels. By 6:00 the various representatives of the parliamentary parties, led by Prime Minister von Acker, had started. The staff car in which Eddie and his British senior colleague were riding, led the cavalcade, followed directly by the prince regent in his car.

At a signal given by us [Eddie recalls] the cars filed out of the rear gates of the Palace, and one by one, at spaced intervals, went to the appointed rendezvous on the outskirts of Brussels. This was done in order not to attract public attention, as the whole trip was to be secret. At the rendezvous, a truck with our food, bedding and all the supplies met us, along with two military police jeeps.

"All the supplies" amounted to, among other items, four days' rations (including coffee) for thirty persons (extra bread to be taken), water-sterilizing tablets, thirty blankets, a large oil stove, cooking utensils and drying cloths, one tow rope, toilet equipment, dusting powder, and eating utensils. Eddie does not reveal how this splendid result of army bureaucratic procedure was stored into one truck.

The cavalcade proceeded via Mannheim to Heidelberg, where without explanation Eddie was left behind. Three days later he was told to proceed, minus the water-sterilizing tablets, the toilet equipment, the dusting powder, *et al.*, by air to Salzburg and thence to King Leopold's hideout in the Alpine resort already made famous in the prewar musical comedy *The White Horse Inn.* But by the time Eddie managed to get there, the king had gone.

For his part in this strange escapade he was given the Belgian Ordre de l'Officier de la Couronne, Leopold II, perhaps, as he wryly speculates, for his part in *not* bringing Leopold back to Brussels.

Several years later, when he finally met Leopold and his common-law wife, the Princesse de Rethy, at a luncheon in New York, Eddie wore his decoration.

It has been said that Eddie Warburg has never had a job in his life, and (except during the war) this is in a sense true. He has seldom if ever held a salaried post and is not a partner in Kuhn, Loeb. However, in the best sense of the phrase, he has made his money work—not only for himself but for others, like his father before him. Today he is one of the seven men who form the board of regents of the State of New York—the only Jew among them. The job of the regents, dating from the time of George Washington, is to supervise all aspects of public education in New York State. The post is unsalaried, time-consuming, and he fills it with the enthusiasm that is perhaps the most salient feature of his character.

Today, as extrovert and gay-spirited as his father, Eddie sits at his desk on the twenty-fifth floor of a Park Avenue office building with a superb view of the East River, dispensing philanthropy and attending to his multifarious activities in connection with the arts of America, chief of which are his duties as Vice-Director for Public Affairs at the Metropolitan Museum of Art.

With his cousin Eric, Eddie is now the chief repository for the family traditions, memories, and anecdotes.

One anecdote concerns his mother Frieda. Eddie's fiancée was not Jewish, and fearful of Frieda's disapproval, it took all of Eddie's courage to introduce them.

Frieda was indeed highly indignant, not because she thought his choice unsuitable, but because she had been the last one in the family to meet her.

Skillfully, Eddie turned away his mother's wrath.

"Yes, I know. But Ma, you never meet the champion until the final."

CHAPTER EIGHTEEN

The Granddaughters
of Moritz

UNLIKE Kipling's Himalayan she-bear, the daughters of
Max, Paul, and Felix Warburg could not be called "more deadly
than the male." On the other hand, in the long history of the
family, no male Warburg (with Sir Siegmund being a possible
exception) has ever exhibited a killer instinct. This easy-going quality has allowed many of the Warburg women to influence the
fortunes of the family from behind the scenes.

Matriarchy has often been a feature of the Warburg story: Sara
Warburg in the nineteenth century ran the family firm through her
two sons. Charlotte, in the succeeding generation, similarly dominated Moritz. Behind the flamboyant figure of Felix stood the
staunch and steadfast Frieda, on whom her children so greatly
relied. Culturally, at least, the mother of the present Sir Siegmund
Warburg had a profound influence on her son. And today most of
her close relatives would agree that Carola Warburg Rothschild
rules the existing American Warburg roost. In discussions with
other members of the family—in Germany as well as in America—an
undertone of awe creeps in when she is mentioned.

It is not difficult to explain why. As the eldest child of Felix and
Frieda she is today the senior representative of the family that is
descended in the direct line from Moritz and Charlotte, and as such

she is inevitably the focus of family loyalty. Moreover, as Felix's daughter and constant companion she has a place apart, for the memory of Felix inspires particular devotion among his children, to say nothing of his nephews and nieces.

Throughout much of her father's life Carola was politically his right-hand woman. While Frieda was taking care of Felix's homes and presiding over his social activities (except when she was turning a tactful blind eye to them), Carola was advising him on his political and international activities—whether he was dealing with the JDC, the creation of the Hebrew University, or his attitudes toward Palestine. She won his complete confidence, even if she could not always control his outbursts. She was at his side as companion-secretary at the Zurich conference of 1936 that sounded the death knell of his political hopes and beliefs.

Carola's mother Frieda has been called the "telephone center" of her family. She was the recipient of many confidences, and she knew—and they were glad that she did—what every member of the family was doing at any time. Carola has to a large extent inherited her mother's mantle of knowledge and discretion. As a result the outsider looking in gets a firm impression that all Warburg roads lead to Carola's Fifth Avenue apartment. All roads except perhaps the road of her cousin Bettina Grimson Warburg.

In one respect Carola and Bettina are alike. Both dislike intrusion into what they consider their private concerns and are hostile to any publicity. Having nothing whatever to hide, they give the totally erroneous impression that they do. But in other ways they are as different as were their respective fathers.

Born in 1900, Bettina Warburg is the only daughter of Paul, father of the Federal Reserve System. Her devotion to his memory and to that of her brother Jimmy is absolute, but her attitude toward her first cousins is somewhat equivocal. She contrasts the charm and benefactions of her uncle Felix unfavorably with what she considers her father's more sterling qualities.

She is very much of a lone-wolf Warburg. It is only with obvious reluctance that she reveals her remarkable qualifications. Gaining a degree in medicine at Cornell University, she chose psychiatry as her calling. Her many posts have included resident psychiatrist of the Westchester division of New York Hospital, instructor at the New York Psychoanalytic Institute, assistant professor of psychiatry at New York Hospital, and resident psychiatrist at New York's Mount Sinai Hospital.

She has been a member (and onetime treasurer) of the American Psychoanalytic Association, the New York Academy of Sciences, the National Committee on Mental Hygiene, and the American Psychosomatic Association. In addition, she was for ten years a member of the New York State Board of Social Welfare, her special care the ten thousand American Indians living in the state.

Perhaps it was her contacts with these underprivileged members of American society, combined with a vital woman's weariness with the routine of committee memberships, that made her seek a more active role in alleviating misery and poverty.

In any event, she resigned from the New York State Board of Social Welfare in 1957 and shortly afterward gave up the active practice of psychiatry. In 1958 she became a member of the board of the Iran Foundation, of which she has been secretary since 1961 and vice-president since 1966.

It is when Bettina Warburg starts to talk about her activities in the latter post that the thaw sets in. Iran has become the love of her life. She spends half of each year traveling among the poverty-stricken villages of the Persian Gulf hinterland and took part in the first malaria-eradication program ever to be set up in Iran. She also helped in the organization of a campaign to increase the amount of protein in the national diet, the development of the Shiraz Medical Center, which now comprises two hospitals and a school of nursing, and the bringing of the first pure water supplies to the villages of the Persian Gulf, made possible by a donation. She personally persuaded the Italo-Persian Oil Company to resuscitate two derelict villages which are now flourishing communities. In all her manifold dealings with the peasants and artisans of the country she has taken as her motto, "Never take a step unless they want it."

Iran has become a second home to this prickly, fascinating woman. She has contributed to its welfare with all her organizing ability and personal contacts and regards herself as an exception to the Warburg family pattern.

"I don't like knowing the right people," she says.

Who could say that of Max, Felix, or even her brother Jimmy? And again, "I prefer their children to my friends."

Of the present Warburg women, she is perhaps the most original and the most admirable.

Bettina Warburg became an American citizen at the age of two, when her father took out his naturalization papers. Her cousin Anita, Max's third daughter, did not settle in the United States until after World War II. Since then, however, she has become an integral part of the New York artistic scene. She adheres far more closely to the American Warburg philanthropic tradition than does Bettina. This tradition is exemplified by the family support of the Institute of Musical Art, by Paul when he rescued the famous Loeb Classical Library from extinction, by Gerald the musician, and by Eddie, the foster-father of American ballet. Today Anita is very involved with the Juilliard School of Music and with the Museum of Modern Art in New York. She has also helped to found in New York the Museum of Contemporary Crafts, the Institute of International Education, and the World Crafts Council, affiliated with UNESCO, which sends American craftsmen to underdeveloped countries.

It was through her connection with the Institute of International Education, and through a chance meeting at a party with the composer Gian-Carlo Menotti, that Anita Warburg found herself visiting the North Italian hill town of Spoleto.

Since the end of World War II "festivals" have sprung up like mushrooms all over the Western world. Often musically based, with other arts in attendance, they are sometimes strangely located. Spoleto, with its narrow, hilly streets, its superb views, its Romanesque cathedral, is a jewel of Tuscany. It is also lacking in the hotel and other accommodations a successful festival needs. Menotti, the inspiration and musical director of this festival, decided to turn a hilltop palazzo into a hotel for his artists. Italian journalists commented, "Menotti must be crazy." The composer's riposte was to announce that the hotel would be called l'Albergo del Mazzo ("the hotel of the insane").

It was into this slightly zany setup that Anita Warburg introduced a group of American students to perform as singers and dancers in—among other entertainments—the chorus of Bizet's opera *l'Arlésienne*. She could not know that the French conductor hired for the occasion would complicate the living space in the smallish hillside town by demanding on arrival the provision of two white horses, a team of dogs, and a flock of sheep. Somehow Anita coped, her students were accommodated, and the opera was performed.

Anita was the first of Max Warburg's daughters to realize what would inevitably happen to her family under the Nazi regime. She went to London in 1935—where in 1940 she married the foreign correspondent of the *Manchester Guardian*, Max Woolf—in the hope that she could act as a bridge between her German parents and American cousins.

In London during World War II she was one of the prime movers in an organization that sent refugees of all nations to jobs throughout Britain when no British worker could be found to fill a vacancy. But her main task during these years was as a leading member of the United Kingdom Search Bureau, charged under the auspices of the Red Cross with finding German, Austrian, and stateless missing persons. Shortly after the war ended she toured the Allied zones of Germany, and as a result of her and her colleagues' activities no less than thirty thousand families were reunited.

There is a pendant to this story. Some years after the war a British corporal stationed in the British Occupation Zone in Germany sent Anita a comprehensive list of what had happened to the Jews of Hamburg.

In the spring of 1971, Anita went shopping in London for a new carpet. The salesman turned out to be the self-same corporal.

Gisela Wyzanski is the youngest of Max Warburg's daughters. She was the favorite of her uncle Aby, and probably of her father as well, a not uncommon condition for the youngest child in a family. Today her lot is cast in the pleasant places of Boston's legal and academic circles, but it was not always so. Like her father, her brother, and her uncle Fritz, in the 1930s she waited out the mounting ferocity of the Nazi blizzard until it was almost too late. In those years Hitler had not yet publicly adopted his "Final Solution"—he appeared bent on extricating Jews from places of power but not at that time on their extermination. It was still possible for them to get out, provided they could raise the very large sums of money needed to buy exit permits (money much needed by the German treasury). In 1938 Gisela was still in Berlin—the last of the family to remain—distributing the funds for exit permits being supplied by rich German Jews, and Jews abroad.

In the autumn of that year the authorities allowed her to go on a fund-raising expedition to the United States. Here was escape and what looked like a sure refuge. In New York were her brother Eric, who had recently founded there his own merchant-banking firm of E. M. Warburg, and her father, still hoping to return to his beloved Hamburg. But, her mission accomplished, Gisela wanted to return to Berlin. Her family, and her American cousins, insisted that she get an immigration permit that would allow her, if necessary, to reenter the United States. To that extent she must take precautions, but once this condition was fulfilled they would raise no objection to her return. They were, all of them, still turning a blind eye to the inescapable facts. The illusion persisted, not only with

Gisela, that a Warburg could somehow still survive in Germany, shunned perhaps but still inviolate and able to help other Jews in the Germany of the autumn of 1938.

The American immigration quota was full, but there was another possibility. On the Canadian quota there were still two vacancies. Gisela crossed the Canadian border and applied for the permit that would allow her to reenter this British Dominion.

Ten days passed, and still no reentry permit. Meanwhile her permit to stay in the United States had expired. Gisela now found herself in a most unwelcome limbo. Then, the Canadians relented, and Gisela got her Canadian permit. The day she received it was November 10, 1938. That night the Nazi authorities launched the infamous pogrom known to history as *Die Kristallnacht*. Back in New York, a still somewhat recalcitrant Gisela was faced by a united family. In America she would now stay. In the climate of anti-Nazi opinion created by the pogrom a permanent visa was easily arranged. In due course she married Judge Charles Wyzanski, and became an American citizen.

Of all living Warburgs, Gisela Wyzanski is, in a religious sense, the most Jewish. She tells how in his last years her father regretted the fact that he had not brought his children up more strictly.

There is a Jewish legend, originating in the *shtetlach* of the poor Eastern European Jews, that God visited all the peoples of the earth and offered to make a covenant with each of them. If they would worship Him and do what He told them, He in turn would give them the Torah and make them "a kingdom of priests and a holy nation." Of all the peoples only one small nomadic tribe in the land of Canaan accepted God's offer. Thus they became the "Chosen" People.

Gisela Wyzanski subscribes to this legend as her grandparents did, but as her father and mother did not. She believes that in a very special sense the Jews are the chosen of God, that they have a special role to play in the world, and that anything that infiltrates into and weakens the essence of Judaism should be eschewed. As a very young woman she became the first of her family wholeheartedly to embrace the cause of Zionism and a national state for the Jews in Palestine. She has seen the latter, secular cause triumph, but if when young she equated Zionism with the pure milk of Jewish orthodoxy, she may well look askance at the Israel of today. Nonetheless she can be called the most Jewish Warburg of them all.

Of Lola Hahn Warburg,[1] Gisela's eldest sister, her father once said: "The first time you meet my daughter she behaves like a lady, the next time she's on at you about her noble causes."

It is unlikely that those who worked with her in the task of helping others will forget her. From the early 1920s Lola Warburg was active in rescuing Jewish children from disaster—initially in providing funds to bring them out of Poland, then the most anti-Semitic of all European countries. Later the emphasis shifted to Nazi Germany, and then to Britain. In 1934 she founded the Children and Youth Aliyah, designed to take the children of German Jews to Palestine. After settling in England, she enlisted the help of Lady Astor, Geoffrey Dawson, then editor of *The Times*, and Norman Bentwich, former chief legal adviser to the British mandatory regime in Palestine. With Bentwich she headed a delegation to the House of Commons. As a result of her intervention in the following years the lives of an estimated ten thousand children were saved.

Later, after World War II was over, Lola fought a battle for seven hundred children from the concentration camps. The British Home Office refused to admit those suffering from tuberculosis. Undeterred, Lola found a hospital in Ashford, Kent, with an empty wing. Into it went the tubercular children. There, and in a hospital in Bishop's Stortford, all were cured.

Lola Warburg's dedication to the welfare of children is not confined to those of her own faith. In the East End of London she

[1] It is the custom in the Warburg family for daughters to resume the family name if their husbands die before them.

worked in close collaboration with the late Sir Basil Henriques, whose famous youth clubs were entirely nondenominational, and she has been equally active in the organization called the "Bridge," founded by Sir Basil's nephew Robert, and whose name indicates its purpose. It supplies funds for exchange visits between British (Jew or Gentile) and Israeli citizens.

Like her uncle Felix, Lola Warburg is an adept fund-raiser. In 1971 she organized an auction at Christie's in London for the benefit of the Save the Children Fund (the successor to the Children and Youth Aliyah). Unfortunately, the auction coincided with a nationwide postal strike. It yielded a profit, nevertheless, of $65,000.

Like Anita and Gisela, Lola was confronted with danger, challenge, and opportunity by the advent of the Nazis. Gisela was lucky to escape going back to Germany. Lola, as the skies over Germany became more lowering, was lucky to be able to leave. Her husband, Rudolf Hahn, was an industrialist with his headquarters in Berlin and a house in the suburb of Wannsee. Like his sister-in-law Anita, and his cousin by marriage Siegmund, he had seen the need to escape while there was still time, but for a man in his position, capable of helping Germany's economic preparations for war, exit permits were not to be obtained. Help came from an unexpected quarter, in the person of Hjalmar Schacht's successor at the ministry of economics. This man coveted the house at Wannsee, and Lola's husband was able to strike a bargain—the house in exchange for an exit permit. The incident, so vital to the Hahns, was typical of the times.

Lola also had a famous brother-in-law. Kurt Hahn was, of course, not a Warburg, but his close connection with them had lasted ever since World War I, when like Max he saw in Prince Max of Baden a possible savior for Germany. In the aftermath of German defeat Kurt Hahn and Prince Max co-founded in a baroque castle near Lake Constance what was to become a world-famous boys' school. The initial institution at Salem has branched out to San Francisco, Greece, Nigeria, Denmark, India; it is represented in the Atlantic College in Wales, and it has become, in Scotland's Gordonstoun, the alma mater of, among others, Prince Charles, the heir to the British throne.

Kurt Hahn brought to fruition, particularly at Salem and Gordonstoun, the doctrine of muscular Christianity propounded in Britain by Dr. Arnold of Rugby in the midnineteenth century. His theories find little favor with today's educators, who tend to believe that hardening the body, far from being a prerequisite to a sane mind, is more likely to stultify it; and even his staunch supporter, Golo Mann (son of Thomas Mann), said on the occasion of Hahn's eightieth birthday: "I fear he has never abandoned the 'Leader Plan' [*Führer-Gedanke*], the education for leadership." [2]

Yet he was a vigorous and courageous opponent of the Nazi regime. It was this opposition that forced him to remove his school from Germany to exile at Gordonstoun in Scotland. Shortly before he left, five Nazi storm troopers trampled a young Communist to death in front of the boy's mother and for this deed received Hitler's public congratulations. Kurt Hahn wrote to all his old and current pupils, demanding that they sever all connections (if any) with the Nazi party, or if not, then with the school in which they had been educated. *Führer manqué*, outstanding educator? There is no doubt in which light the Warburgs viewed him, and during Hahn's exile in England they always found a warm welcome at Gordonstoun.

[2] *Suddeentsche Zeitung*, May, 1966.

❦ CHAPTER NINETEEN

Collateral Warburgs

As HAS already been seen, this family, which traces its antecedents back for over four hundred years to the day in the early sixteenth century when Simon von Cassel sought and gained admittance to the town of Warburg, has spread its activities and influence over many lands and many professions. If for no other reason than space, this book has concentrated (with the single exception of Professor Otto Warburg, the Nobel prize winner and one of the family's chief adornments) on the direct descendants of Moses Marcus and Gerson, the founders of the firm of M. M. Warburg & Sons in 1798. These decendants have grown and prospered, first in Germany and then in America, and much later, in the person of Sir Siegmund Warburg, in Britain. There are, however, many "collateral" Warburgs stemming from Simon von Cassel who have also bestowed distinction on the name.

There was, for example, Dr. Emil Warburg, father of Professor Otto and an outstanding physicist who became head of the Physikalische-Technische Reichsanstalt in Berlin, and another Otto, professor of botany at Berlin University, who donated to the Hebrew University in Jerusalem the first collection of tropical plants ever to be established in what was then Palestine. It later became a minor counterpart of the botanical collection at Kew Gardens, England, and another Warburg institute—of tropical agriculture—may be set up in Israel in memory of his achievements.

Dr. Otto's chief significance in the Warburg story is that he was the first in the family wholeheartedly to espouse the cause of Zionism. He succeeded Theodor Herzl as president of the World Zionist Organization.

In Scandinavia, Professor Carl Warburg has made his mark as a philologist and a leading authority and author of a book on the Swedish language still used in all schools in Sweden.

Professor Erik Warburg of Copenhagen is one of the most famous heart specialists in Europe. Before World War II he was also private physician to the king of Denmark. When the Germans occupied the country in April, 1940, he became active in the Resistance movement. He was arrested and thrown into prison, but King Christian intervened. Unless the professor had constant access to him, the king protested, his life would be endangered. Perhaps Hitler had read his Shakespeare: "there's a divinity doth hedge a king"—provided the king resists. In any event, King Christian was granted his request and the professor lived for the rest of the war in the Amalienborg Palace in Copenhagen, reporting to the Gestapo twice a day. After 1945 he became head of Denmark's largest hospital and chancellor of Copenhagen University.

There still remain the "British" Warburgs. Sir Siegmund was a comparatively late arrival. In the nineteenth century several members of the collateral branches of the family emigrated from Scandinavia and settled in different parts of England. Britain was at the time less plagued by anti-Semitism than the United States, the only other destination they considered. But however assimilated these British Warburgs became, like their German and American counterparts they have always retained an intense family allegiance.

In the southwesternmost corner of Wales there lives a Warburg by another name. Edmund Speyer is the son of Olga Warburg, sister of the "Famous Five." His career has been as varied as it has been checkered and fascinating. His mother had married Paul

Kohn-Speyer, the chairman of the famous metal-brokerage firm of Brandeis-Goldschmidt. She died a few weeks after Edmund's birth. He was brought up, in his own words, to be more British than the British, in a large, friendless house in London's Lennox Gardens, then the haunt of the haute bourgeoisie. As a boy he was a brilliant student, winning a scholarship to Charterhouse School and choosing to enter Balliol College, Oxford, because of the high reputation of its concerts. Once again the musical motif reappears in the Warburg story, reminiscent of Gerald and of Edmund's remote ancestor, the Danish Pius, who played quartets with Brahms.

He was for a year a trainee with his uncle Max in Warburgs in Hamburg, then returned to London to try, and fail, at the law. In 1928, at the age of twenty-four, he joined his father in Brandeis Goldschmidt in expectation of a partnership that never materialized. In 1929 he went to New York as internal auditor for the National Lead Company, later traveling for the firm on a westward trip around the world.

On the eve of World War II he was commissioned in the Royal Air Force, serving as an intelligence officer in Pembrokeshire (England), West Africa, and Ireland. Later he became a member of the interallied special legal unit at SHAEF and was mainly responsible (his legal training coming belatedly into use) for drawing up the special laws later put into effect for the postwar occupation of Germany. After a spell as a member of the Control Commission for Germany, he was demobilized on the very day on which the sale to an American company of Brandeis Goldschmidt, already gravely damaged by the high death duties payable on Edmund's father's death in 1942, was engineered by his cousin Siegmund.

Edmund Speyer's career had been peripatetic and not altogether successful. Subsequently he was to illustrate the versatility of the Warburg clan by adding yet another occupation to the list already given. In faraway Pembrokeshire he became a highly successful farmer and country gentleman (his eldest son has recently taken over the farm). He is on the council of the Country Landowners Association, he was chairman of the local rural district council in the year of Prince Charles's investiture as Prince of Wales, and he is currently a member of the Pembrokeshire Water Board and chairman of the local cooperative wholesale society. Ironically, since Edmund Speyer professes no admiration for his cousin Siegmund's handling of the affairs of Brandeis Goldschmidt, the investments of the cooperative movement are handled by the firm of S. G. Warburg and Co.

Abandoning in middle age the world of big business and finance, Edmund Speyer is the first of the British Warburgs to become part of the "landed gentry."

Another outstanding example of the "British" Warburgs is Maurice Magnus Warburg, born in Stockholm in 1841, who was for a while a well-known merchant and later Swedish vice-consul in Leeds, England. Maurice eventually returned to Sweden, but his son settled permanently in London, bearing the defiantly British Christian names of Gordon and Percy.

Then there was Frederick Elias Warburg, born at Göteborg, Sweden, in 1832, who came to London as a young man in about 1860 and remained there all his life. He joined Sir Ernest Cassel in financing the Tuppenny Tube, the first subway to be constructed in London.

One of his sons, Oscar, became chairman of the London County Council and was a member of the court of the University of London, besides making a name for himself as a writer on botany. One of *his* sons, following in his footsteps, became professor of botany at Oxford University. Oscar, after receiving the accolade at Buckingham Palace, became the first Warburg knight.

❧ CHAPTER TWENTY

Fredric: The Publisher

In a lighthearted article published some years ago in *The New Yorker*, the Fredric John Warburg of Secker & Warburg (London) wrote:

The astonishing fact about the London Warburgs—at least about those who are still living—is that they are *poor* Warburgs. . . . There's been no "million dollars at a clip" given away to deserving causes by London Warburgs these last fifty years, though around 1912 my aunt Agnes presented to the nation part of Boxhill, in Surrey, where George Eliot lived. . . . Can not the financially red-blooded Warburgs of New York stop ignoring their financially anemic, if talented cousins?

It is hardly surprising that on his next visit to New York his reception by his American cousins was somewhat chilly.

It was not until after the end of World War II that any Warburg who had made his home in Britain showed anything approaching financial genius. Certainly Frederick Elias, Fredric's grandfather, amassed wealth out of the "Tuppenny Tube." It was difficult for anyone associated with Sir Ernest Cassel *not* to make money. But one of his sons, at least, frittered away most of his share of his father's fortune. John Simon Warburg is listed in the Warburg genealogical tree as just "A Private Man." According to *his* son, the sharp decrease in the family's fortune was due to John Simon's steady refusal all through his life to do any work.

THE WARBURGS

That son was, and still is, Fredric John Warburg, and no one could level that accusation against him. Certainly the outstanding member to date of the older British branch of the family, Fred, as the world knows him, was born in 1898 and given the orthodox upper- or upper-middle-class education provided then by Westminster School and Christ Church, Oxford. Orthodox, too, was his army service as a second lieutenant during the closing stages of World War I. After that, however, orthodoxy took flight. Fred's subsequent career was very turbulent, full of ups and downs, of challenges to the "Establishment," of triumphs—and of failures too—but inspired always by a passionate interest in the world of books. This passion was to make him, along with only a few other contemporaries such as his particular rival Victor Gollancz, a publisher of rare force, imagination, and courage.

In Fred's eyes, Gollancz was, with his Left Book Club (which Fred regarded as little more than a supplement to *Pravda*) a fellow traveler of the Communist party, almost a stooge for the Russians, right up to the Nazi-Soviet Pact and outbreak of war in September, 1939. The two men could agree on the evils of fascism, but Fred could not forgive Gollancz for his blindness to the almost equal menace to freedom of thought and speech implicit in Stalinist Russia.

Fred's dedication to the cause of books enabled the firm of Secker & Warburg, of which he was the principal founder and chairman, to acquire great prestige, but Fred would be the first to admit that he lacked the financial acumen possessed by so many previous Warburgs, and in particular by his cousin Siegmund. His grasp of the economics of publishing was almost as slender as that of his two chief colleagues, Roger Senhouse and the author of this book. Together, on at least one occasion, the three brought the firm to the brink of disaster.

Fred started his publishing career with the solidly based educational firm of Routledge & Kegan Paul, Ltd. Success came quickly, and while still in his thirties he became its managing director. But disaster was to follow—in an attempt to brighten up the firm's image, he pressed for the creation of a fiction list. To his senior colleagues this smacked of rank heresy. Rapidly Fred found himself out on his ear. Undaunted, he determined to strike out on his own. He did so with the slenderest of financial resources and with a partner with whom, apart from the love of books, he had very little in common. Going for a song (to be precise, £3,100) in 1936 was the immensely prestigious but now insolvent firm of Martin Secker. Fred and Roger Senhouse bought it and soon found themselves in financial peril. Somehow, on two occasions, more money was raised, and the new firm moved on into the wartime period when the demand for books so greatly exceeded the supply that it was hard for publishers not to make profits.

In the early prewar days Fred raised defiantly aloft the banner of Trotskyism, at that time in Britain hardly a passport to financial success. Yet by doing so, he attracted to his list one of the most significant authors of the century. In 1938 Secker & Warburg published *Homage to Catalonia* by George Orwell, after it had been turned down on ideological grounds by Victor Gollancz as being too anti-Russian. It made no one's fortune. Rather, up to the date of Orwell's death in 1950, it showed "in the red" on the firm's balance sheet. But it was the precursor of two novels famous today the world over. If he had published nothing else, *Animal Farm* and *Nineteen Eighty-four* would have assured Fred Warburg an honored position in the publishing hall of fame.

But he published a great deal else. In the years after the war, he attracted to his growing but still small international list authors like Colette, Angus Wilson, Günter Grass, William L. Shirer, Alberto Moravia, and Lewis Mumford (who had followed him from Routledge). Few observers of the literary scene knew that his firm was not prospering financially. In fact it was nearing a liquidity crisis, and in 1951 the storm broke. Perhaps for the first time in history a Warburg in business found himself without any money or credit! It was not a matter of "giving away a million dollars at a clip," but of desperately searching for £20,000, and at the pinch, no fellow Warburg was willing to ante up.

At this moment another remarkable publisher came to the rescue. A. S. Frere was chairman of the prosperous firm of William Heinemann, Ltd. In the face of considerable opposition from his colleagues he offered an umbrella under which Fred and his colleagues could shelter. He would invest money in the stricken firm, take over financial control, but leave editorial policy entirely in the hands of his beneficiaries. From that moment, though there were still bumpy passages ahead (caused by its chairman's occasionally overweaning optimism), Secker & Warburg, now with the benefit of sound financial advice, never really looked back. There were, of course, the skeptics who at first maintained that a giant had swallowed a minnow. With immense panache Fred silenced these doubters, managing in the process, at least with many of his American colleagues, to convey the impression that he was conferring a benefit on Heinemann by associating them with his list.

Allied with his optimism was Fred's willingness to take risks. A prime example of this quality occurred shortly after the Heinemann rescue operation, when Secker & Warburg was offered a fascinating but wholly unauthenticated autobiography of an alleged Tibetan lama who called himself T. Lobsang Rampa. Ignoring the warnings of several Tibetan experts that the book was a total fabrication, Fred, sensing a best-seller, published. The experts were right. The lama proved to be a man named Cyril Henry Hoskins, the son of a Devonshire plumber, who had never been nearer Lhasa than London. But by the time Hoskins was unmasked, *The Third Eye* had sold fifty thousand copies in Britain (as well as many thousands in America and Germany), and after the exposure it continued to sell almost as well.[1] There are still readers of this book as well as people who have met its author who refuse to believe that it is a fake. T. Lobsang Rampa is as plausible in the flesh as he is on the page.

---

[1] *The Third Eye* is still, in 1973, in print in paperback.

The villain, perhaps, of that piece, Fred was certainly the hero of another. In 1953 Secker & Warburg published an American novel called *The Philanderer*. It is tempting to say that he took a calculated risk here too, by publishing what might be attacked as an obscene novel, but in fact it did not at the time of publication occur to him or his colleagues that it was in the least "dirty." Six months passed, during which it sold a modest three thousand copies. Then a single copy found its way into the hands of a straitlaced young policeman on the Isle of Man. The policeman reported to his superiors that the publisher should be prosecuted for "obscene libel."

The wheels of the law grind exceeding slow, and it was not until six months later that a somewhat embarrassed detective sergeant, accompanied by a constable, appeared in Secker & Warburg's office to announce that proceedings would be taken against the firm of Secker & Warburg, its chairman, and the book's printers. In almost every previous case of this nature—the legal term "obscene libel" means in layman's language too much and too explicit sex—the publisher had pleaded guilty and been fined in a magistrates' court, rather than face the ordeal of trial by jury in the British High Court of Justice. The age of permissiveness was still a long way ahead. No publisher had ever been acquitted on this charge, but Fredric Warburg accepted the challenge, even though it meant his appearance in the dock at the Old Bailey and the possibility of going to prison—the fate of at least one other previous publisher. However, he and his firm were triumphantly acquitted, and as a result of the publicity this rather undistinguished and by today's standards totally innocuous novel rapidly sold twenty thousand copies. Many of its purchasers must have been sadly disappointed by what they read.

The verdict of "not guilty" in the *Philanderer* case changed the course of publishing history in England. It was the second in a series of five such prosecutions launched in that year by a straitlaced director of public prosecutions with the backing of a similarly minded home secretary. The first publisher pleaded guilty in a magistrates' court. Fred Warburg chose to fight, and the other three followed his example, only one being convicted. In his summing up in the *Philanderer* case Mr. Justice Stable asked:

> So far as his [the chief character's] amatory adventures are concerned, the book does deal, with candour or if you prefer it crudity, with the realities of human intercourse. There is no getting away from that, and the Crown [the prosecution] say that is sheer filth. Members of the jury, is the act of sexual passion sheer filth? It may be an error of taste to write about it. It may be a matter in which old-fashioned people would mourn the reticence that was observed in these matters yesterday. But is it sheer filth? [2]

With these words the judge dragged the law of obscenity, kicking and screaming a little, into the contemporary world. In addition, his rhetorical question sparked off an agitation to change the law, led by that champion of what initially seem lost causes, Sir A. P. Herbert. This agitation penetrated Parliament and led to the passing of a new act that made literary merit a defense to any charge of obscenity. More important, perhaps, Fred Warburg's stand, the judge's summing up, and Sir A. P. Herbert's agitation changed the whole climate of public opinion.

Fredric Warburg went into semiretirement in 1971, becoming nonexecutive president of the company he had founded. He left it at a peak not only of prestige, an asset it possessed throughout his career, but of profitability as well. Through the years he has perhaps mellowed. The banner of Trotskyism no longer flutters at his masthead. He started, self-confessedly, as a "political" publisher; he ended as a publisher of worthwhile books. He tends now to oppose whichever party is in power, a modified form of his initial and never dimmed enthusiasm for freedom of thought and speech. But against the version of Communism practiced by Stalin and his

[2] Reprinted as a pamphlet by Secker & Warburg, 1954.

successors he has remained throughout, like his favorite author George Orwell, an implacable foe.

Fred has always stood a little apart from the Warburg clan. His cousins have a visual, clearly Jewish resemblance to each other that he does not share. His is an almost classical countenance, with its long face, straight nose, crinkly, close-cropped hair. In moments of anger or frustration he looks like an arrogant Assyrian preparing to attack a sheepfold. It is a splendid performance belying a character essentially sympathetic to criticism and even outright opposition.

As if to demonstrate that versatility which is such a marked feature of the Warburg strain, Fred fathered by his first wife, a son who became British and then world champion at the esoteric game of court tennis. David Warburg added yet another to the long list of Warburg occupations.

To the gallery of Warburg women, Fred added in 1932, his second wife, Pamela de Bayou. This strikingly handsome, warm-hearted, and totally uninhibited dress-designer and painter deserves a book to herself. Her reputation for indiscretion is legendary in London literary circles. Few realize that she is indiscreet for a purpose. If Fred does not conform to the general Warburg pattern, Pamela conforms to no pattern whatsoever. Throughout Fred's publishing career, she has shown him a loyalty so fierce and un-compromising as to be sometimes embarrassing to him and to others. On occasion in talking to her about Fred, one feels the Almighty is under discussion; but such loyalty is a rare and won-derful thing.

❧ CHAPTER TWENTY-ONE

The Warburg Legacy

Documentation is scanty about the early Warburgs. From the records of *Stadt* Warburg we know that from comparatively humble beginnings they prospered in a modest, and certainly discreet, manner, and that in the seventeenth century they began to expand their operations. In the eighteenth century they moved to Danish Altona where they found the business and cultural climate more equable, more conducive to money-making, than could be enjoyed anywhere in Germany. But it was not until 1798 when Marcus Moses and Gerson incorporated the firm of M. M. Warburg and Sons that they emerged from comparative obscurity. Since then they have proved themselves a family rich in attainments and individually remarkably successful in many walks of life.

The nineteenth century was a period of consolidation. Always respectable, the Warburgs became respected. They made good marriages, M. M. Warburg & Co. expanded, if slowly, for the dynamism of matriarch Sara was not matched by her younger son Moritz, who after his mother's and brother Siegmund's deaths, had to take control. Yet Moritz is perhaps *the* key figure in the Warburg story, for his wife Charlotte gave him five sons four of whom each in his different way brought the family international status and fame.

George Warburg, Sir Siegmund's father, admitted the Warburgs "have had their ups and downs." [1] They would have been less fascinating both as individuals and as a family if it had been otherwise—that is, if their onward march had been unimpaired.

Of the "Famous Four," Aby the eldest descended for a time into the abyss of insanity—only to recover and increase his international fame during the last years of his life.

Max guided the family firm to a pinnacle of success but was forced to witness its takeover by the Nazis and spent the last years of his life in exile. Yet he lived long enough to see the destruction of the enemies of his race, and under his son Eric the firm was reestablished and prospered again.

Paul died in the lengthening shadow of the Wall Street crash and the resultant financial panic that swept the United States, of which he had so vainly warned, but had it not been for his brainchild, the Federal Reserve System, the disaster would have been far worse. He did not live to see his only son, Jimmy, emerge as an architect of financial recovery as well as a liberal-minded figure in national politics, but Paul's posthumous fame is perhaps greater than that of any other Warburg to date.

Felix died a disappointed man, his vision of what a Jewish "home" in Palestine should be shattered by his Zionist opponents, but his achievements—above all, the Joint Distribution Committee and all it still means to Jews in peril all over the world—have stood the test of time.

Of the next generation Jimmy can be regarded, at least politically, as a failure. His "downs" were decisive, his "ups" temporary only. Yet the range of his activities in other fields—in literature, finance, real estate, the theater—were more far-ranging than any other Warburg has so far attempted. Only the present Sir Siegmund has had no failure attached to his name. If at some time he should suffer a defeat, the smart money will be on his survival.

[1] Joseph Wechsberg, "A Prince of the City," *New Yorker*, 9, April 1966.

THE WARBURGS

In his reflections on Warburg "ups and downs," Siegmund's father was obviously referring primarily to finance. How rich were and are the Warburgs?

It is impossible to ascertain the wealth of any individual Warburg. A *New Yorker* "profile" said that when Paul died in 1932, he was worth $2.5 million.[2] His brother Felix was reputed to be much richer—his wealth stemmed from his position as a partner in Kuhn, Loeb rather than from any conscious effort to acquire it.

No really hard figures are available, but it is safe to assume that of the "Famous Four," Felix was very rich indeed, and Max and Paul were rich by any normal standards. All three owned at least two houses, though of course Felix's town and country mansions were far greater than those of Paul in New York and at Greenwich, Connecticut, and of Max in Hamburg and at Kösterberg. All kept substantial households—Felix employed sixteen servants.

Much of this wealth rubbed off on their children. When Edward, Felix's only surviving son, entertains visitors at his eleven-acre home in Westport, Connecticut, they are accommodated in a separate guest house, complete with dining and sitting rooms, a patio with a heated swimming pool, and an indoor tennis court. At Kösterberg too, Eric's guests can be accommodated in separate houses. But time—and some diffusion of wealth—marches on. In New York, the Fifth Avenue mansion has given way to Edward's Park Avenue apartment, and in the city of Hamburg there is no longer a Warburg residence. The younger generation's establishments have withered somewhat as well. Live-in servants are few, replaced by small flocks of maids who come in for the day. But the change in life-style is due much more to the fashions prevailing in the postwar world than to a decrease in the supply of money the Warburgs can command.

After all, ever since Simon the moneylender arrived in Warburg four hundred years ago, money has been in the Warburg blood.

[2] Geoffrey T. Hellman, "A Schiff Sortie . . . ," *New Yorker*, 11, June 1955.

Wealthy they have been, but never in their long history—except, perhaps, for Felix—ostentatiously so. Of the Warburgs described in this book, many were singularly uninterested in *making* money for themselves, or in banking per se. Aby, Felix, perhaps the American Frederick, spring to mind, and collaterally the Nobel prize winner, Otto. With the exception of the occasional "poor Warburg," like the British Fredric, it is true that they had no need to be motivated to make money. Financially, they were well cushioned. Jimmy Warburg's closest friend told the author that Jimmy had made three separate fortunes in his lifetime, adding, "None of them was really necessary."

Not necessary, but time and again, in the best sense of the word, very useful. When Warburgs have consciously pursued the amassing of money—and however good some of them have been at it—they have done so not as an end in itself. At first it was a way of purchasing security in a largely hostile world; when this had been achieved, it was a means to ends they have wanted to foster.

Without his family's fortune Aby could never have laid the foundations of his world-famous library, nor could it have been sustained in its new English home without the family's support. Without the fortune that accrued to him through his marriage and resulting partnership in Kuhn, Loeb, Felix could not have become one of the outstanding philanthropists of his generation, a patron of much that is best in New York's cultural tradition. Without his established financial position and money sense Jimmy could not have played so valuable and independent a role on the American political scene. Without inherited money his sister Bettina could never have rescued so many Persian villages from the abyss of poverty, nor could Bettina's cousin Lola have pursued her own charitable aims.

Charitable bequests are not, of course, peculiar to the Warburgs, nor to those of the Jewish faith in general. But the attitude of Jews toward money does differ in one respect from that of most Christians. Nothing in their religion inhibits them from the fullest bestowal of monetary favors—whether on individuals, causes, or institutions—*in their lifetime.* Nor are they under the compulsion that many devout Christians feel to put their church in the forefront of their charitable interests. In the sense in which the pope or the archbishop of Canterbury mean the words, they have no real church and no strong sense of an afterlife. It is what they do while they are alive that is all-important.

Felix's benefactions, Aby's founding, with the family's financial assistance, of the Warburg Institute, Felix's support, and later Jimmy's and Edward's, in sustaining the Institute of Musical Art, Frederick's financial assistance to American youth movements and Bettina's to Persian villages must be seen in this perspective. No Warburg would claim to wear a philanthropic halo. To most of them philanthropy is second nature and has nothing to do with atonement for ill-gotten gains or with seeking a reward in heaven, possible motives behind the setting up of many great charitable foundations by rich white Anglo-Saxon Protestants. By their actions, both as individuals and as a family, the Warburgs have demonstrated that money can be the root, not of all evil, but of much good.

For over a century, as the lives and careers of its individual members have spanned the world, the Warburg family has been a family united in diversity.

Operating from manifold telephone numbers, the individual family members need a "central exchange" to keep them in contact with one another. Since the family branched out from Germany in the latter half of the nineteenth century, there has been one woman in each generation who has taken over that vital function. First it was Charlotte, then Frieda, and today, Carola.

Members of the family may, on occasion, disagree with one another, but with the aid of these powerful female figures at the family center, when confronted by an outsider they close ranks.

There is no doubt that these family ties are intensified by their Jewishness. Although many individual Warburgs are only nominal practitioners of Judaism, are not necessarily keen advocates and supporters of the State of Israel, and maintain strong loyalties to the countries in which they live, they are nonetheless bound together by the transcendent fact of being not just a family, but a Jewish family.

But how typical are they of Jewry today? In his controversial book *The American Jews,* James Yaffe seeks to establish certain stereotypes for the Jews of America. These stereotypes may not find general favor with either Jews or Christians. They are perhaps too sweeping in their scope. But in relation to the Warburg family, they have their fascination.

Yaffe quotes the Gentile writer Hutchins Hapgood, describing the attitude of an immigrant Jewish boy at the turn of the century: "At the same time that he is keenly sensitive to the charm of his American environment, with its practical and national opportunities, he has still a deep love for his race and the old things." [3]

Commenting on this passage, Yaffe refers to "that split personality which runs through all of the American Jew's history. . . . This split personality is the key to understanding American Jewish life." [4]

Paul with his fond memories of his boyhood home in Germany is an example of an American Warburg who retained throughout his life a deep love for "the old things." Felix, on the other hand, adopted wholeheartedly his new country, from the very beginning. Yet it was Felix, not Paul, who became the first Warburg to interest himself in the plight of Jews all over the world, and in the nascent state of Israel.

Jimmy, Bettina, Edward, Carola, Gerald, and "Piggy" are all examples from succeeding generations of American Warburgs who have followed in Felix's footsteps. While being very much a part of the American scene, they have also, in their different ways,

[3] *The American Jews* (New York: 1968), p. 19.
[4] *The American Jews,* p. 19.

expressed their loyalty to their Jewish heritage. A "split personality," in the case of individual Warburgs, has proved no handicap.

Yaffe also refers to a general Jewish fear that all Gentiles are
anti-Semitic and a consequent desire to placate them, adding that
"all the same, deep down in his heart, the Jew feels sure that his
efforts to placate the Gentiles are doomed to failure . . . [so] they
isolate themselves as much as they can from the Gentile world." [5]
Here Yaffe may afford us an insight into the family's collective
history both in the United States and in Europe. Although the
record proves conclusively that the Warburgs have mingled freely
with the Gentile world around them in their day-to-day affairs,
becoming just as much citizens of Germany, the United States, and
Britain as they are members of the Jewish race, there has been a
pattern among the family's most eminent members to avoid becoming public figures—in other words a reluctance to seek or accept
public recognition, sometimes even public responsibility. One
thinks of Paul's hesitation about accepting President Wilson's appointment to the Federal Reserve Board, for example, or Max's
refusal to head the financial delegation of a defeated Germany to the
Versailles peace talks. Whether modesty and a desire for privacy
supply the whole answer, or Yaffe's theory of a fear of reprisal for
success is another possible motive for this puzzling behavior, is of
course impossible to finally judge.

And the present attitude of the Jews toward Germany?

Yaffe believes that

The basic attitude [of a large number of Jews] can be expressed very
simply: all Germans are Nazis. This applies just as much to those who were
in their teens or younger during the war, to those who weren't even born
when Hitler died. . . . This generalization has a corollary. No Nazi ever
stops being a Nazi. The poison has no antidote—neither time, nor remorse,
nor religious conversion. For this reason Germany must be watched from
now until the end of time. . . . [6]

[5] *American Jews*, p. 63.
[6] *American Jews*, p. 57.

To this despairing, vengeful, Old Testament view, most War-burgs do not subscribe. We have seen the reaction of Gisela's nine-year-old son when questioned for having said that Hamburg was the best place in Europe. There is no desire for this fearful revenge in the heart of his uncle Eric. Nor do the Warburgs indulge in that other Jaffe charge, Jewish anti-Semitism. "Self-hatred, in fact, is a word often used to describe a common phenome-non—Jewish anti-Semitism," Yaffe says,[7] which leads, he believes, to Jews making anti-Jewish jokes at each other's expense. The War-burgs make jokes about each other, but never anti-Jewish jokes about anyone.

The Warburgs, then, contradict as many of the Jewish stereo-types which Yaffe adumbrates as they exemplify. If they maintain multiple loyalties, they do so without conflict. They are by no means introverted or self-hating. If they harbor any fear of the Gentile world, it does not take the form of isolating themselves from it. They do not, most of them, regard the possible advent of neo-Nazism as a matter for eternal vigilance. They have pride above all of family. It is significant that in Yaffe's book their name appears only once, and briefly, in a purely philanthropic context.

Yet in one other important respect the American Warburgs do conform to a Yaffe pattern. Unlike those German Jews who emi-grated from Germany in the aftermath of repression following the 1848 uprisings, the Warburgs were part of a group of unforced immigrants that filtered into the United States over a fifty-year period. Their immediate predecessors were the Guggenheims, the Morgenthaus, the Lehmans, the Lewisohns, the Schiffs—into whom they married. All these families crossed the Atlantic westward, not because they were being persecuted but because opportunity was beckoning. It beckoned because America was the land of financial opportunity, apparently unbedeviled by Jew-baiting, and above all a land of the bourgeoisie, and it was in that category that these German-born financiers and businessmen had always belonged.

[7] *American Jews*, p. 71.

The Warburg family arrived in New York more by marriage than design, yet they shared the views of their predecessors. They wanted to be accepted by this new land of promise, and in large measure the German families of this new voluntary Diaspora have succeeded in their aim—as have their British counterparts.

It is unlikely, however, that they ever would have succeeded had they not rid themselves of the trappings and tenents of Jewish orthodoxy, so ardently followed, for example, by Moritz and Charlotte Warburg, which proclaimed the Jews the Chosen of God, or in other words, a race apart. The Reform Movement was one solution. Represented by the famous Temple Emanu-El in New York, of which Felix Warburg became so staunch a supporter, and where his close friend Judah Magnes was for many years the chief rabbi, the aim of the Reform Movement was to supply a philosophical justification for complete assimilation into the Gentile world, and take the Jewishness out of Judaism.[8]

Acceptance was an ideal consistently pursued by the American Warburgs; as it was sought by British Jews—the Rothschilds, Samuels, Cohens, or the Sephardic Henriques. It was sought, perhaps unconsciously, by Max Warburg in Germany. But how successful were these Jewish families in general, and the Warburgs in particular, in becoming accepted?

The Warburgs have traveled very far along that road, but not the whole way. Perhaps complete acceptance is a will-o'-the-wisp, and between Gentile and Jew there will always be a measure of arrière-pensée.

But this can be said: In Britain Sir Siegmund Warburg, Fredric Warburg, and Edmund Speyer are British in thought and deed as well as by nationality. In Germany Eric, like his father before him, is a German first and a Jew second. In the United States the descendants of Moritz and Charlotte regard themselves as American citi-

---

[8] In Israel today, this struggle between orthodoxy and liberalism is still unresolved.

zens in the fullest sense, despite certain pressures, applied to all the chief American-Jewish families, to transfer their allegiance to the State of Israel. That a great many Warburgs in all three countries devote much time, money, and energy to Jewish affairs, including the affairs of Israel, presents no contradiction to this attitude.

Of all the great Jewish clans that have sprung into prominence in the last century and a half, the House of Rothschild and the Warburg family can claim to be the most outstanding. Their financial fortunes have been closely interrelated, with the Rothschilds showing the way—at least until very recently. Young Warburgs have served their apprenticeships *chez* Rothschild, and vice versa, and a comparison of the two houses is inevitable.

The Rothschilds represent the patrician element in Jewry; the Warburgs, the haute bourgeoisie. The Rothschilds abound in barons; the Warburgs can only boast two knights. The Rothschilds live in châteaus; the Warburgs live in houses. There is no vintage wine called Château Mouton Warburg. Rothschild entertainments are lavish, studded with stars of stage and screen, with pretenders to thrones and other discarded royalties. The Warburgs are no slouches at hospitality, but they prefer family affairs, on the occasion of an anniversary of some kind to give their entertainment point. In 1970 there was the celebration of Eric Warburg's seventieth birthday at Kösterberg, Germany. In 1971 Lola Hahn Warburg's threescore years and ten were similarly marked at Stratford-on-Avon. In 1972 it was the turn, jointly, of Gisela Wyzanski and Eric's wife Dorothea, the place again Kösterberg.

This comparison of the style of entertainment the two families engage in may seem trivial, redolent of the gossip column. Yet it has its relevance. The Rothschilds have become the most "accepted" of all Jewish families in Europe by virtue of an acquired arrogance born of their astonishing financial successes. The Warburgs possess no such extrovert quality. They seek neither publicity nor glamour.

Their hospitality is a private affair. It makes for a great difference between the two families—particularly with regard to public opinion.

The descendants of Simon von Cassel have traveled very far since the day the prince-bishop of Paderborn gave Simon permission to practice the trades of "money changer, pawnbroker, and lender of funds against grain." They have become prominent in many walks of life, preeminent in some. Today they are citizens of many lands. If they are not the subject of gossip columns or society pages, it is due more to a question of style than to an absence of spectacular achievement. A fitting description of them all is that they have become citizens of the world.

❧ Epilogue

LET the last word rest with Germany, where the Warburg family grew from small beginnings to fruition and fame. The estate of Kösterberg slopes steeply down to the River Elbe, three hundred feet below. One of the highest points in the flat North German plain, it commands a superb view over the wide-flowing river, filled with seagoing traffic passing to and from the docks of Hamburg. It is situated in the suburb of Blankenese, fifteen miles northwest of the city.

Hamburg, of course, has grown greatly since the day Moritz bought Kösterberg at the turn of the century. Its suburbs now reach almost to the Warburg gate. But in many ways the city retains its old attractions. Though badly bombed in World War II, its center, built around the Alster lakes, remains miraculously intact. Nowhere else in Germany today is the foreigner less inclined to an attack of claustrophobia. Nowhere is it easier to forget that Hitler ever existed. Hamburg has retained its previous atmosphere, typical of much that is best in Germany.

The estate of Kösterberg comprises several houses and a sizable acreage, but it is simply labeled Number 60 in its street. In some ways this modest appellation is typical of the Warburgs.

The children of the "Famous Four" are reaching or passing their allotted span of threescore years and ten. Eric Warburg was not in

1970 the eldest of them. His cousin, the American Frederick, was his senior by two years (he died in 1973). But Eric is regarded by all the family as the personification of Warburg unity in diversity, and in 1970, at his beloved Kösterberg, he celebrated his seventieth birthday.

Assembled on that occasion were Warburgs old and Warburgs young—the latter looking a shade askance at the intensity of the family atmosphere by which they were surrounded, for they could know little of what many of their elders had endured in the recent past.

There was Eric's own family and cousins from Germany, Britain, the United States, and Scandinavia. They had come to greet the man who had returned to the family birthplace and restored the position and prestige of the firm that Moses Marcus and Gerson had founded.

The presence of the mayor of Hamburg and representatives of every aspect of the great city's life—Jew and Gentile alike—made the birthday party not only a celebration in honor of a remarkable man but a demonstration that wherever else anti-Semitism might still lurk in the shadows, it found no place in the great city in which the Warburgs had lived for more than a century and a half.

The celebration took place in a fiberglass tent designed by Eric's prospective son-in-law, in a garden ablaze with rhododendrons, azaleas, and laburnum. Shortly afterward, at another reception in the same setting, the Warburgs celebrated yet another family occasion—the marriage of Eric's elder daughter Marie to Haase von Blücher, a collateral descendant of the famous field marshal who with the Duke of Wellington had been a victor of the Battle of Waterloo.

Marie's great-uncle Aby had been the first Warburg to defy the family taboo on marriages to Gentiles. Other Warburgs have followed Aby's example. It is inconceivable that Marie will be the last. The Warburgs have always moved with the times.

Epilogue

Earlier in 1970 had occurred the redress of a wrong that had persisted for over thirty years. In 1936 the firm of M. M. Warburg & Co. had been "Aryanized." Since Eric's return to Germany after World War II he had been its effective head, but its title had remained Brinckmann Wirtz & Co. In 1970, after prolonged negotiations, the name of Warburg was restored to the firm's letterhead. The firm's full designation is now M. M. Warburg, Brinckmann Wirtz & Co.

What's in a name? In this case a great deal, for this merchant banking firm, famous the world over, is now known once more as "Warburgs."

❧ Selective Bibliography

Agar, Herbert. *The Saving Remnant: An Account of Jewish Survival.* New York: Viking, 1960.

Birmingham, Stephen. *Our Crowd.* New York: Har-Row, 1967. London: Longmans Green, 1968.

Burns, J. McGregor. *Roosevelt, the Lion and the Fox.* New York: Harcourt Brace Jovanovich, 1956. London: Secker & Warburg, 1956.

Cecil, Lamarr. *Albert Ballin.* Princeton, N.J.: Princeton University Press, 1967.

Clapp, Edwin. *The Port of Hamburg.* New Haven, Conn.: Yale University Press, 1911. London: Oxford University Press, 1912.

Gombrich, E.H. *Aby M. Warburg.* London: The Warburg Institute, 1970.

Keynes, J.M. *The Economic Consequences of the Peace.* New York: Harcourt Brace Jovanovich, 1920. London: Macmillan, 1920.

Morton, Frederick. *The Rothschilds.* New York: Atheneum, 1961. London: Secker & Warburg, 1964.

Rosenbaum, Edward. *M.M. Warburg & Co.* London: Leo Baeck Institute Yearbook, Vol. VII, 1962.

Sampson, Anthony. *Anatomy of Britain Today.* New York: Har-Row, 1965. London: Hodder & Stoughton, 1965.

Schlesinger, Arthur. *The Age of Roosevelt.* New York: Houghton-Mifflin, Vol. 1, 1957; Vol. 2, 1959; Vol. 3, 1960. London: Heinemann, 1959.

Shirer, William L. *The Rise and Fall of the Third Reich.* New York: Simon & Schuster, 1960. London: Secker & Warburg, 1960.

Warburg, James P. *The Long Road Home.* New York: Doubleday, 1964.

Wechsberg, Joseph P. *The Merchant Bankers.* Boston: Little, Brown, 1966. London: Weidenfeld & Nicolson, 1967.

Weizmann, Chaim. *Trial and Error.* New York: Harper Brothers, 1949. London: Hamish Hamilton, 1949.

Yaffe, James. *The American Jews.* New York: Random House, 1968.

❧ Index

Index

Index

223, 247; "Aryanization" of, 117–18, 124; during nineteenth century, 25, 47–48, 234; prior to economic depression, 109–10
M. M. Warburg, Brinckmann Wirtz & Co., 247
Moley, Raymond, 159–60, 162
Mond, Sir Alfred, 97
Money Muddle, The (James P. Warburg), 154, 162
Morgan Grenfell, 60
Morgenthau (family), 241
Morton, Frederick, 19–20
Murphy, Robert D., 202
Mussolini, Benito, 167, 168

Napoleon Bonaparte, 22–23, 43, 201
Neurath, Baron von, 116, 177, 178, 179
New York City Ballet, 205, 206–08
New York City Board of Education, 70
New York State Board of Regents, 212
Niemeyer, Christian, 124
N. M. Rothschild & Co. *See* Rothschild (firm)
Nuremberg Laws of 1935, 113–114

Oppenheim (family), 26, 30, 34, 35
Orwell, George, 229, 233
Our Crowd (Birmingham), 95, 198
Our War and Our Peace (James P. Warburg), 165
Owen, Robert, 61

Palestine, 95–96, 99, 101–02, 106–07
Panofsky, Erwin, 129
Papen, Franz von, 111
Pauli, G.,129
Peel, Lord, 106
Philanderer, The, 231–32
Polaroid Corporation, 159

Portal, Viscount, 180, 181
Project Hope, 203
Proust, Marcel, 47

Raskin, Marcus G., 172
Rathenau, Walther, 75, 82
Reform Movement, 242
Reichsbank, 112, 113, 114, 158
Reichstag fire, 113, 178
Reinhardt, Max, 99–100
Rockefeller Foundation, 151
Roosevelt, Franklin D., 61, 159–60, 161–64, 165, 167, 168, 169–70
Roosevelt, James, 159
Roosevelt, Theodore, 60, 87
Rosenbaum, Edward, 25, 50, 111, 121
Rosimer, James, 204, 205
Ross, Sir Denison, 145–46
Rothschild, Alphonse, 32
Rothschild, Baron, 32
Rothschild, Carola. *See* Warburg, Carola
Rothschild, James de, 97
Rothschild, Lord (1891), 45
Rothschild, Lord (1944), 209
Rothschild, Mayer, 19–20
Rothschild (family), 19–20, 24, 32, 36, 49, 242; compared with Warburg family, 243–44
Rothschild (firm), 23, 25, 44, 54, 90, 177, 186
Rothschilds, The (Morton), 19–20

Saint Moritz, reunion of Warburg brothers at, 80
Salem School, 221–22
Samuel Montagu (firm), 37, 57
Sassoon (family), 49
Saving Remnant, The (Agar), 94
Saxl, Fritz, 145, 147
Schacht, Hjalmar, 80–81, 112, 113, 114, 116, 117, 118, 159, 221

Index